First published in Great Britain by Artus Books Ltd

This 1984 edition is published by
British Heritage Press, distributed
by Crown Publishers, Inc.

© 1979 Mark Girouard

ISBN 0-517-44646-4

Printed in Hong Kong

hgfedcba

Every effort has been made to provide
accurate information regarding opening times
etc. of the houses included in this book, but
they do change from year to year, and it
would be advisable to check with the house
itself before a visit.

endpapers An early eighteenth-century view of
Uppark by the Dutch painter Pieter
Tillemans.

opposite The armoury, Hatfield House.

overleaf Looking through the gates of the great
forecourt of Blenheim Palace to the towers
looming in the mist.

HISTORIC
HOUSES
OF BRITAIN

HISTORIC
HOUSES
OF BRITAIN

MARK GIROUARD

BRITISH HERITAGE PRESS
NEW YORK

CONTENTS

3 PERSONAL REFLECTIONS

4 IN TRUST FOR THE NATION

Introduction

It is often said that there is nothing like the English (or for that matter the Scottish or Welsh) country house. It has become a cliché, but it is worth pausing to think what makes country houses so unusual. Country houses, incidentally, should not be confused with mere houses in the country. They are houses which, at least when they were built, had a large estate attached to them: not just one farm but several farms, and often many thousands of acres. One quality which houses of this kind have in abundance, and almost exclusively, is that the same family has lived in many of them for generations. This may seem a cliché too but it is as well to consider just what it means. Most houses, even if they last a long time, change owners at regular intervals, and the new owners chuck out everything that was left behind by the old ones. It is quite rare for someone to live in what used to be their parents' house; and even rarer for them to live in their grandparents' or great-grandparents' house. But many country houses in Britain have been lived in by the same family for hundreds of years – in some cases (Berkeley Castle for instance) for over eight hundred years. This means that they tend to contain the leavings of many past generations – leavings of all kinds, not just pictures and furniture, but the clothes they wore, the toys they played with, the letters and bills they received, the diaries and accounts they kept, the pots and pans in their kitchens and the carts, carriages and cars in their stables and garages. Of course a great deal is thrown away even in an old country house, and progressively less survives of the earlier generations. But one asset these houses always have is space; the people in them have tended to banish unwanted objects to upstairs rooms, outhouses or cupboards, rather than throw them away altogether. And their contents don't suffer from that most destructive of all operations – moving house.

A house which retained the belongings of many generations would always be fascinating, whatever its size and whatever type of person had occupied it. But country houses have this additional interest, that the people who lived in them were often famous people, and almost always people who played a leading part in the neighbourhood. Until comparatively recently, they were the houses of the people who ruled the country. For many centuries the only people who had real and lasting power were those who owned land in large quantities; and anyone with ambition automatically tried to acquire as much land as he could, and at least one country house to go with it.

This meant that most country houses were not just quiet backwaters; they were places where things happened. Prime ministers, the trusted advisers of kings, the great merchant princes who ran the country's economy, all lived in country houses as well as in the town. People of importance, from the king or queen downward, came to stay with them. The future of Britain was discussed, and sometimes decided, by small groups walking along the garden terraces or the galleries of country houses, or sitting over their wine for long hours after dinner. In the smaller houses, if national affairs weren't being settled, local ones were; for in the days when London bureaucrats were almost non-existent, and local authorities in the modern sense entirely so, the squires in their manor-houses ran the neighbourhood with almost despotic power.

So when visiting country houses one can get a vivid sense of being in on the action – even if the action took place many centuries ago. They have yet another dimension however, because they existed on so many levels. Famous people may have lived in them, but so did their wives, their mothers-in-law, their children, their servants and their dependants. A big country house was a community made up quite often of more than a hundred people, living, working, intriguing, playing and gossiping together. Moreover, the community extended beyond the household to a large number of people who, in some way or other, were tied up with the great house: there were the poor relations who came to stay whenever they could; there were the tenant-farmers whose rent supplied most of the family's wealth; there were the bailiffs, shepherds, herdsmen and farm workers who ran or worked on the farms which the family farmed themselves; the rangers, keepers and foresters who supervised their deer parks and forests; the masons, carpenters, thatchers and painters, who built or maintained all the many buildings on their estates. There was a large circle of hangers-on, supporters or local tradespeople who had put themselves under the protection of the great house, or were hoping to get custom or favours from it. All of these were constantly coming and going, and many were regularly fed at the house even if they did not sleep there. And if servants and estate-workers left no personal relics in the house, their equipment and uniforms are often still there – the great mangles which they turned in the laundries, the spits which they worked in the kitchens, the livery coats which the footmen wore, the shovel-boards on which they amused themselves in the long evenings, the regulations written up for their attention in the servants' hall.

So country houses can provide one with a huge slice of life, stretching over many centuries and through many classes, from people whose names are household words to the boy who helped the gardener or the maid who whipped the cream; and because so much has survived it is a slice of life that can be recreated and envisaged more vividly than any other portion of our past.

Another fascinating aspect of these houses is that they have constantly – if slowly – changed. The slice of life which they present is a slice with different layers in it, and every layer has a different flavour. To be able to recognize these changes, to distinguish layer from layer and understand how things worked at one period and were adapted to make them work at another, makes visiting country houses a much more exciting and rewarding affair than just walking round them looking at room after room filled with different objects.

Let us imagine, for instance, Great Gumblestone Hall, somewhere in the Midlands. The Gumble family have been living there since the Middle Ages and the pride of the house is the magnificent oak-ceilinged great hall which Sir Guy Gumble built in the late fourteenth century. But the Gumbles have long since stopped eating at their high table on the dais, with their household down in the body of the hall below them. Since those days the hall has undergone various changes; it finally became a huge sitting-room to accommodate the house-parties given by Edwardian Gumbles. Comfortable, shapeless sofas and armchairs with chintz skirts down to the ground are now dotted all over it, mixed up with writing-tables, a grand piano, and a round table which used to be set up for afternoon tea in front of the huge old fireplace.

The winding stone staircase which originally led from one end of the hall was replaced in Jacobean days, when Sir Gervase Gumble employed some London carpenters to build splendid new stairs of carved oak, with a lion at the top of every post holding up the Gumble crest. The staircase led up to Sir Gervase's great chamber on the first floor, embellished with tapestries, an elaborate plaster ceiling and at one end a great bay window. Here Sir Gervase used to dine in state; he had his own private orchestra which blew a fanfare on its trumpets and oboes as each course was carried up the great staircase, led by his gentleman usher carrying a white staff-of-office.

On more everyday occasions Sir Gervase and his lady used to eat downstairs in his panelled parlour underneath the great chamber; only the servants ate in the hall. But after a time, carrying the food up to the great chamber began to seem too much of a business, especially as it was stone cold by the time it arrived. The room

Black and white cupids and fancifully dressed dancers perform to an orchestra in Elizabethan times, to entertain Sir Henry Unton and his guests. Such entertainments were often put on for special occasions in the halls and great chambers of country houses from the middle ages to the seventeenth century.

8

left The painted staircase at Knole in Kent was inserted into an older house in the early seventeenth century. Carved and painted wooden staircases were a new invention of the period, and replaced traditional winding stone staircases in many houses. As at Knole, they provided a stately route by which both dinner guests and the procession of servants carrying each course could mount to the great chamber on the first floor.

right The Prince of Wales (second from the right) smoking a cigar with Lord Armstrong (in the top hat) on the terrace before Cragside in Northumberland. Lord Armstrong, a typical self-made man of the nineteenth century, made a great fortune from the manufacture of hydraulic machinery and armaments. At Cragside he built himself a romantic gabled and castellated house surrounded by hundreds of acres of pine woods on the edge of the moors. Until the 1890s it had no smoking room and even the Prince of Wales had to smoke outdoors; to smoke in the living-rooms of a country house was unthinkable.

gradually fell into disuse; in the end it was turned into a library when Bishop Gumble (a younger son) died in about 1800 and left the family his great collection of theological books, which nobody ever read.

Meanwhile, in the early years of the eighteenth century, the first Viscount Gumble had built a grand new range facing the garden along one side of the hall. It had a saloon in the centre for meals and receptions with a great pillared portico in front of it; to either side were two matching suites, each consisting of a withdrawing-chamber, a bedchamber (with a great four-poster bed crowned with ostrich feathers), a closet for study and prayer, and a room for a servant. The viscount and his wife lived in one of the suites and the other was kept for important guests. All the doors were aligned and the viscount boasted that they were so beautifully made you could look through all the keyholes at once, from one end of the building to the other. From the garden you would scarcely have guessed that you were looking at the same house, so different was its portico and symmetry from the rambling gables and haphazardly arranged windows on the entrance side. The viscount would have liked to rebuild the whole house, but he didn't have the money.

A Gumble wife in the late eighteenth century brought with her as a dowry a market garden on the edge of London; and in Regency days the vegetables gave way to houses – Gumble Square, Gumble Street and Gumblestone Crescent. The rents from these helped to pay for the great Gumblestone house-parties of the nineteenth century. First the turnpike roads and then the railways made it easier and easier to gather twenty or thirty people for a week or a weekend. All sorts of changes took place at the Hall. The rooms to either side of the saloon in the eighteenth-century wing were knocked together to make a big new dining-room and drawing-room, and the four-poster beds were moved upstairs. The old

Elizabethan parlour became a billiard room for the gentlemen, and a new smoking room was built on beyond it, together with a gunroom, cloakrooms and what became known as the bachelors' staircase, leading up to six little bedrooms for visiting bachelors. The servants were moved out of the attics to make way for the twelve Gumble children and their nannies and governesses.

The servants had long ago ceased eating in the hall and sleeping next door to their masters and mistresses, or on little truckle beds in their bedrooms, as had happened up to the sixteenth century. Now they were tidied away on their own in an enormous new servants' wing built round two courtyards to one side of the hall. Here they had their own servants' hall, a pantry for the butler, a snug sitting-room for the housekeeper and a rabbit warren of larders, laundries, store-rooms and rooms for brushing boots and filling oil-lamps. A long row of bells outside the servants' hall kept them in touch with the Gumbles and their guests. At the end of the furthest court a steam-engine puffed away pumping water up into the new water-tower, and a gashouse piped home-made gas to the village as well as the Hall. Steam-engine and gashouse are still there, although disused since the house went over long ago to electricity and the mains.

Today the Gumbles would probably have moved into one end of the house and opened the rest to the public. Alternatively they might have sold it for conversion into a school; or handed it over with an endowment to the National Trust, and retired to the dower house. Many country houses open to the public are still privately owned. The families who live in them hold on to them through pride and affection, often at a considerable financial sacrifice to themselves; but more and more families are finding the struggle more than they can bear. This is where the National Trust can step in and take over a house (and sometimes the old owners become tenants and continue to live there). The service rendered by the Trust in saving houses which would otherwise have been sold and possibly demolished can scarcely be exaggerated.

The houses that follow are all open to the public. The first section deals with three royal buildings, one of which – Sandringham – is still lived in by the queen. The second and fourth sections deal with privately owned houses and houses belonging to the National Trust. The third section is based on a different kind of classification; it consists of houses, of both types of ownership, which are especially associated with one person rather than a family. In general, the houses are scattered all over England, Scotland and Wales, and have been selected so as to give a wide variety of date, size and character.

above The family and servants of Sir John Boileau assembled on the lawn in front of Ketteringham Hall, Norfolk, in about 1850. Sexes were carefully segregated even for a photograph.

above right Edwardian servants grouped round the butler and housekeeper at Erddig Hall, Clwyd. For more about the servants at Erddig see pages 159–162.

right A servants' dormitory of the 1830s on the attic floor at Mamhead in Devonshire. The beds were designed to fold away into the recesses. Curtains used to hang from the top rails to provide a degree of privacy.

far right Eighteenth-century regulations in the servants' hall at Hatchlands, Surrey. Such boards used to hang in many servants' halls. Rule 10 shows that the water supply of the house was distributed from an upper cistern into which water was pumped by hand. Other eighteenth-century houses had pumps powered by water-wheel, donkey-wheel, or even steam.

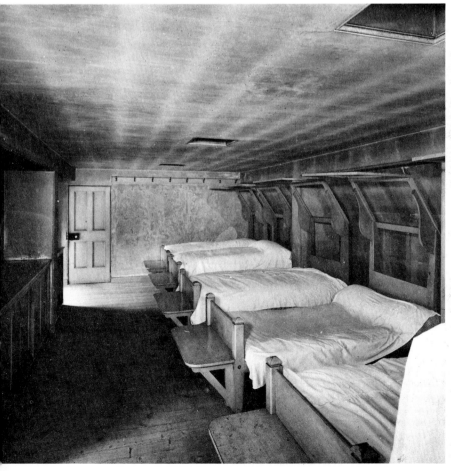

1 ROYAL RESIDENCES

Hampton Court Palace
Greater London

In the seventeenth and eighteenth centuries kings were at the height of their glory. All over Europe they acquired more and more power, so that in France Louis XIV could announce, with splendid effrontery: 'I am the state.' One of the ways they showed their power was in their palaces. Versailles is and always was the most famous example, but Versailles was only one of hundreds of palaces that sprang up like mushrooms all over Europe. It wasn't only kings and emperors who built them; every tin-pot German prince or Italian grand duke had to have his own version of Versailles, complete with fountains, avenues and interminable vistas in all directions.

The English kings ranked very low in this palace-building league, but not for lack of trying. At various times they had plans on the grand scale drawn up for new palaces in Whitehall, Greenwich, Richmond, Hyde Park, Winchester, Kensington and Hampton Court; but they could never raise the funds to build them. This failure was a direct result of their inability to make themselves all-powerful monarchs on the continental model. To do this they had to control parliament, but parliament refused to be controlled. Charles I tried, and lost his head; James II tried, and lost his throne.

So when James II's daughter Mary and her Dutch husband and co-monarch William took over the crown in 1688, their palace-building ambitions were quickly cut down to size. William had asthma, and London smoke made him feel ill. He deserted his great palace in Whitehall for Kensington, which was still just outside London, and Hampton Court, which was right in the country.

preceding pages The east front of Hampton Court, designed by Christopher Wren for William and Mary in 1689.

above Looking from the gardens into the park through a wrought-iron gate of the late seventeenth century.

left The gatehouse showing the Tudor brickwork and chimneys of the time of Cardinal Wolsey and Henry VIII.

There was an old Tudor palace at Hampton Court, but the royal architect Sir Christopher Wren drew up plans for replacing it with a splendid new palace on the Versailles model, approached by a mile-long avenue across Bushey Park. It was all a pipe-dream; the Bushey Park avenue was the only part of it to materialize. Instead, Wren had to content himself with remodelling two sides and one courtyard of the old palace. The result is what one finds there today.

It is hard to regret the failure of Wren's grand design. Europe is full of would-be Versailles, but the Tudor and Stuart mixture of Hampton Court is unique. One sets off the other. The Tudor parts are mellow, rambling, plum-coloured and romantic; the Stuart ones are trim, red and white, and as neat and regular as soldiers on parade. One keeps going from one to the other, looking down from big seventeenth-century windows into little secret Tudor courtyards, or finding a stately row of Christopher Wren's columns drawn up in front of the old brick walls and battlements of the Tudor palace.

The original Hampton Court was not built as a royal palace, but as the enormous country house of Cardinal Wolsey. Wolsey had been a clever poor boy, the son of a butcher in Ipswich. He went into the church, which in those days was the best and almost the only way for a poor boy with ambition to get on in the world. He succeeded so well that he ended up as Bishop of Durham, Abbot of St Albans, Archbishop of York, Lord Chancellor, Henry VIII's chief minister and a cardinal – all at the same time. He had a huge house in London, four splendid houses in the country and about five hundred servants. In 1514 he acquired the land on which Hampton Court stands and started building straight away. By the 1520s the entertainments he gave there were the talk of Europe. The butcher's son was living as magnificently as a king, and clearly enjoying it.

However, when Henry VIII was endeavouring to get rid of his first wife, Katherine of Aragon, Wolsey failed to arrange an annulment and fell out of favour. Falling out of favour with Henry VIII was a frightening experience. In 1529 Wolsey made a desperate attempt to save his life. He presented Hampton Court and everything in it to the king. It did him no good; in 1530 he was arrested for high treason. He would almost certainly have lost his head if he had not died on his way to London to stand trial.

So Wolsey moved off the stage at Hampton Court, and Henry VIII moved on, so effectively that although Wolsey was responsible for at least half of the surviving Tudor buildings there is little to remind visitors of him, not even a portrait. But Henry VIII's bluff, bearded face looks out with slightly sinister joviality from every corner.

Wolsey's house was built round two big courtyards (the present Base and Clock Courts) and a number of smaller ones. Henry added a third large court, rebuilt Wolsey's hall, remodelled his chapel, and added and altered in all directions. The palace as he left it was an extraordinary combination of chaos and order, squalor and splendour. The idea that important buildings should be regular and symmetrical was only just beginning to catch on in England. The entrance front is more or less symmetrical, and the gateways that join the main courtyards line up neatly with each other; but to one side of them is a rabbit warren of little, secret, surprising courts with evocative names such as the Lord Chamberlain's Court, the Master Carpenter's Court, the Fish Court and the Chapel Court. The rooms that were demolished to make way for Wren's buildings were grander in scale, but arranged even more chaotically – a tangle of turrets, bay windows and unexpected projections, surmounted by fantastically twisted and ornamented brick chimney-stacks. Many of these still stand on the surviving portions of the Tudor buildings, and are one of the most memorable features of Hampton Court. The whole huge complex swarmed with people – around a thousand occupied it when the king was there. They ranged from splendidly dressed courtiers and sober government officials to kitchen scullions, who were ordered in 1526 'not to

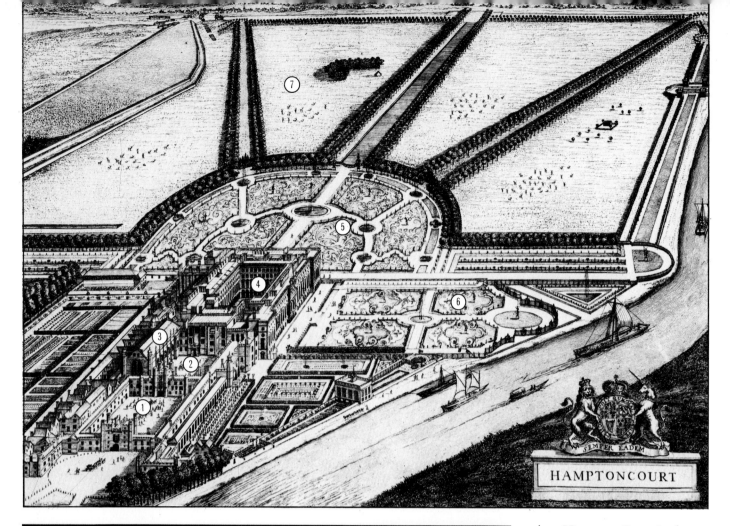

HAMPTONCOURT

above Hampton Court in the early eighteenth century. The buildings and general layout have scarcely been altered since. 1. Tudor Base Court. 2. Tudor Clock Court. 3. Henry VIII's great hall. 4. The Fountain Court, round which Christopher Wren remodelled the east end of the palace. 5. The Fountain Garden. 6. The Privy Garden. 7. The Home Park.

left Cavernous fire places in Henry VIII's great kitchen. There were no stoves in the sixteenth century; all roasting and boiling was done on open fires, in front of which huge spits were rotated by half-naked kitchen boys. In the foreground are charcoal braziers originally used to warm rooms in other parts of the palace.

Looking up into the roof of Henry VIII's great hall.

go naked or in garments of such vileness as they now do, or sleep night and day in the kitchens by the fire side'.

The cavernous Tudor kitchens at Hampton Court survive almost unaltered, along with remains of their original equipment. So do the beer-cellars (all foreign visitors in the sixteenth century were impressed by the vast quantities of beer drunk by Englishmen) and the vaulted wine-cellars next door to them. Outside the kitchens is a roomy lobby with rows of serving hatches opening into the kitchens. Here the beefeaters or yeomen of the guard (who were Henry VIII's invention) assembled in their colourful uniforms to collect the dishes for each course, and march with them in procession up the adjacent stairs to the great hall or to Henry VIII's presence chamber beyond it.

The great hall is the most splendid surviving relic of Henry VIII at Hampton Court. Its glorious roof manages to turn the relatively simple business of bridging a span of forty feet into an exciting escape into fantasy. It is like a combination of the hold of a great ship, the skeleton of a whale, and the stalactited roof of a cave – but a cave rich with colour and ornament as well as stalactites. In its main structure and much of its decoration it is in the tradition of the great timber roofs built across halls and churches in the later Middle Ages, but the cherubs and other ornament with which it is covered represent the latest Renaissance fashion, straight from France or Italy.

The same kind of enjoyably extravagant mixture is to be found in the ceiling of the chapel royal (this looks like stone, although it is in fact wood), from which rows of cherubs blowing trumpets are suspended as though in the observation baskets of balloons. It can also be seen in the simpler ceiling of the 'watching chamber' next to the great hall, and in two ceilings in what are now known as Wolsey's closet and Wolsey's chamber. The latter are in fact the only interiors to survive from Wolsey's time. Their ceilings are as rich and intricate as the clothes of Henry VIII and his courtiers, which were embroidered with gold thread and sewn with pearls, as shown in contemporary portraits.

left The queen's drawing-room. The cut-velvet state bed was made for Queen Anne. On the wall to the right, her husband Prince George of Denmark points to the British fleet.

right The chapel royal. The gilded roof was made for Henry VIII in 1535–6, but almost all the fittings date from the late seventeenth century. The reredos behind the altar was designed by Christopher Wren and carved by Grinling Gibbons.

Although Henry VIII's household ate in the hall, he himself only made comparatively rare appearances there; he ate, slept, danced and received visitors in a long series of sumptuously decorated rooms which started beyond the watching chamber (so called because the beefeaters kept watch there). All these have gone, as have the almost equally sumptuous rooms occupied in succession by Henry's numerous wives, in which the wretched royal craftsmen found that as soon as they had carved one set of initials, mottoes and coats of arms, they had to knock them out and start carving another.

There is one surviving memento of his fifth queen Catherine Howard: the gallery outside the chapel is said to have been haunted by her ever since she ran screaming down it in 1542. She was running away from the soldiers who had come to arrest her, and trying to get to the king in the chapel to beg for his mercy; but she never reached him, and lost her head shortly afterwards for alleged infidelity to her husband. Life in the Tudor Hampton Court was colourful but also dangerous. It is so picturesque and peaceful today that one tends to forget its more sinister associations.

Wren's new rooms were intended to fill much the same functions as Henry VIII's, only brought up to date. Royal marriages were invariably dynastic alliances rather than love matches, and it was taken for granted that kings would have mistresses. King and queen accordingly had self-contained apartments, approached by separate staircases and with separate bedrooms. These apartments were divided into two quite different parts. In the state part their occupants dined, received ambassadors, bestowed knighthoods, attended balls on royal birthdays and showed themselves to their courtiers, all in lofty and richly decorated rooms with splendid fittings. Their private (or 'privy') lodgings were reserved for their family or their lovers, and for private meetings to discuss important or secret business; they were approached by little separate back stairs, as important in their own way as the grand staircases which led to the state rooms.

By Wren's time what had been rather haphazardly arranged in Tudor days had become more organized. Room was expected to follow room with clockwork precision, and doors and corridors lined up with each other, so that royalty and other great people, attended by lords and gentlemen-in-waiting, could progress tidily through the state rooms or along lofty galleries to services in the chapel. Royal people were made to seem almost superhuman by the great canopies flaunting ostrich feathers which were hung over the chairs of state and the state beds, and by painted walls and ceilings on which they were depicted swathed in amorphous draperies and lolling on clouds among gods and goddesses.

The king's staircase leads up to the king's state rooms along the south front, and was completed in about 1700 for William of Orange. The frescoes are by the Italian Antonio Verrio. On the main wall a row of Roman emperors are being threatened with punishment for their misdeeds – a reference to the supposed misdeeds of the later Stuarts, whom William had forcibly displaced.

However, the state rooms at Hampton Court suffered from shortage of cash, like all other royal projects at the time. The craftsmen working on them often had to wait ten or twenty years to be paid. Work proceeded very slowly; Queen Mary died long before her own rooms were ready, and the queen's staircase was only finally decorated in 1735, nearly fifty years after work on the state apartments had started. Many of the rooms never got the painted ceilings planned for them. As a result of this and the length of time involved in decorating them, they lack the unity of character and concentrated sumptuousness that seventeenth-century state rooms aimed for. Moreover, when the royal family stopped living there in the mid-eighteenth century, a good many of the contents were removed to other palaces.

Even so, the rooms contain plenty of good things – elaborate state beds and canopies, splendid chairs covered with faded silk or embroidery, portraits of kings and courtiers of every description, Italian paintings of the highest quality and towering gilt mirrors with tarnished silver-backed glass winking sleepily between the carving. In the king's guard room (the Stuart equivalent of Henry VIII's watching chamber at the other end of the palace) the walls are lined with a sensational display of nearly three thousand arms, arranged in patterns by William III's gunsmith. There is plenty of delicate woodcarving by Grinling Gibbons, the greatest master of his art, both in the state rooms and the chapel royal. The king's and queen's staircases, the queen's drawing-room and the king's and queen's bedchambers have wall or ceiling frescoes painted by the Italian Antonio Verrio, and the Englishmen Sir James Thornhill and William Kent. These are full of propaganda or compliments, expressed in terms of Greek and Roman history and mythology. The boisterous romp of gods, goddesses and others that sprawl over walls and ceiling of the king's staircase are a concealed attack on the Stuart kings (shown as Roman emperors) in favour of William of Orange (shown as Hercules). The absurd cherub being pulled along in a shell in the queen's drawing-room symbolizes the love between Queen Anne and her husband George of Denmark.

Perhaps the most attractive of Verrio's frescoes is the least ambitious, the ceiling of the little room now known as the king's dressing-room. Here Mars and Venus disport in a setting of cupids, turtle-doves, parrots, and orange trees in tubs. This room was originally the king's 'little bedchamber', and its function was part of a royal way of life which seems incredibly remote today. State bedchambers were not at all private rooms. Kings and queens received visitors in them; when they married they were publicly put to bed in them, and the court processed through to see them in bed together; their getting up in the morning was an elaborate ceremony, in which as late as 1761 rival earls were quarrelling as to who should help the king on with his shirt. But from the late seventeenth century onwards there was an increasing tendency for state bedchambers to be used only for ceremony; the king, having been solemnly installed in the state bed by the great officials of his court, got out of it and retired into a smaller bedroom next door.

The two unassuming rooms through the little bedchamber were planned as the king's closet and the queen's closet. They mark the junction of the two apartments and were intended for private reading, visiting and meetings. There are more private rooms at the back of the queen's apartment, looking on to the courtyard. They are not at all large and are completely unpretentious. The very much larger queen's gallery, which joins her closet to his, was also a private room. It was the favourite room of George II and his wife; they used to take breakfast there together, play cards, drink chocolate and talk to their friends. Even in its half-furnished state today one can see why they liked it; although large, it is a friendly room flooded with light and it looks out over the gardens instead of rather pokily on to a courtyard.

In spite of the contents of the royal apartments, it is perhaps the views across the gardens which are their most memorable feature. The best view of all was given to the queen's drawing-room; by the end of the seventeenth century the state drawing-room was the centre of court life and so it was placed in the middle of the main palace front, looking on to the Fountain Garden. It is the only room in which the windows go right down to the floor, and through them one looks along three radiating avenues to the trees and water of the Home Park.

The Hampton Court gardens were laid out at the same time as Wren's palace ranges were being built, and on the same regular lines. The same craftsmen worked on both; the Huguenot ironsmith who made the railings of the king's and queen's staircases also made the superb wrought-iron gates in the gardens; Grinling Gibbons carved garden urns and statues, as well as limewood festoons in the state rooms. So palace and gardens are all of a piece, and the formality of the gardens is a perfect foil to Wren's stately but friendly façades. There is something wonderfully peaceful about their long vistas, clipped yew trees, wide open spaces, tumbling fountains and broad gravel walks. One reaches them through the echoing cloisters of Wren's Fountain Court, which is always cool, even in summer; strolls up and down the paths, talks to the ducks on the canals, looks through the great wrought-iron gates at the deer in the park, or leans on the railings at the end of the Long Water and watches the motionless line of fishermen failing to catch fish along its banks.

In various corners of the gardens are special features, all worth a visit (although the gardens are infuriatingly organized in a series of cul-de-sacs, so that one always seems to walk twice as far as one expected). They include William III's banqueting house; the great vine, planted in 1769, the main branch of which is over a hundred feet long; the real tennis court where Charles II and Henry VIII played tennis; and the famous (if rather moth-eaten) maze, first laid out in the reign of Queen Anne.

When George III was a boy, he had his ears boxed in public at Hampton Court by his grandfather George II. He felt so humiliated that he took a permanent dislike to the place. He never lived there when he became king, and no king or queen has lived there since. Queen Victoria opened the gardens and royal apartments to the public; the rest of the palace was divided into 'grace and favour' apartments, where the widows of peers and distinguished public servants polished their husbands' medals, gossiped with the other old ladies, and hauled their food in baskets up Wren's back stairs to the upper floors.

May–September: weekdays 9.30–6, Sunday 11–6. November–February: weekdays 9.30–4, Sunday 2–4. March, April and October: weekdays 9.30–5, Sunday 2–5. Closed Good Friday, Christmas Eve–Boxing Day and New Year's Day.

The Royal Pavilion
Brighton

In 1750 Dr Richard Russell published a book in which he announced a startling new discovery: dipping the body in salt water helped cure certain diseases. A rush to the sea began which has never stopped. At first it was entirely for medical reasons. Invalids were seized and dipped in salt water by muscular female 'dippers' and 'bathers'; some even drank hot salt water mixed with milk and cream of tartar. But soon a visit to the sea became a new form of fun for the English upper classes. Jaded and stuffed after the rich dinners of the London season, they packed their bags and led the simple life for a while by the sea.

The fishing village of Brighton was conveniently close to London, and became the most fashionable of the new resorts. Life there was chic, dashing and extremely enjoyable. It centred round the Steine – a great open space of grassland next to the village, on which the fishermen dried their nets. After their morning dip dukes and duchesses strolled round the Steine, looked at the fishermen, met other fashionable friends and listened to the band playing outside the new circulating library. In the evening they danced in the Assembly Room which had been added on to the Castle Inn by the Steine.

Soon people began to build or rent houses round the Steine. The Duke of Marlborough had a house there. So did George III's dissolute brother the Duke of Cumberland. The latter's nephew, the young Prince of Wales, came to stay with him and fell in love with Brighton – and with, as a contemporary put it 'the angelic figure of a sea-nymph whom he one day encountered reclining on one of the groins of the beach'.

Such 'sea-nymphs' came to Brighton in large numbers, hoping to be picked up by fashionable gentlemen. The prince's nymph was Charlotte Fortescue, as dumb as she was beautiful. The prince soon left her for the great love of his life – Mrs Fitzherbert. This devout young Catholic lady, highly respectable and already twice a widow, would only associate with him if he married her. He knew that he would never get permission from his father for an official marriage to a Catholic and a commoner, so in 1785 he married her secretly in her own drawing-room. The prince's debts had recently been paid for him by parliament, and he had promised to live within his income. He sold his racehorses and brought Mrs Fitzherbert down to Brighton, full of good resolutions to live a life of idyllic simplicity in a cottage.

He settled, in fact, in a little house which had once been a farm, two up and two

below The Pavilion as enlarged to the designs of Henry Holland in 1787. The wing to the left, with its two bow windows, is the original cottage into which the Prince Regent moved in 1786.

right The Pavilion as further enlarged by extension at either end in 1801–3. The foreground shows the busy social life of the Steine, the open space where fishermen dried their nets when Brighton was still a fishing village.

bottom right The Pavilion as transformed to the designs of John Nash in 1815–22. The outlines of Holland's earlier building can still be seen beneath oriental domes and verandahs.

down, looking over the Steine to the sea. But the prince was incurably extravagant. The simple life became less and less simple. Bit by bit the lovers' cottage grew into the bizarre but beautiful Royal Pavilion – one of the most extraordinary buildings in the world.

The first change came in 1787. A large circular saloon crowned by a dome was built on to one end of the cottage, which was duplicated beyond it. Two wings were built out at the back. The cottage had become an elegant mansion in the classical style. The Prince came there whenever he could. He collected a circle of gay, hard-drinking friends and gave some wild parties; but Mrs Fitzherbert was always a restraining influence, and the dissipations of the Pavilion have been much exaggerated. Her reign was briefly interrupted by the Prince's loveless and disastrous official marriage with a German princess in 1795; George III made the marriage a condition of paying his son's debts. The prince showed little interest. 'One damned *frau* is as good as another,' he remarked. The marriage soon broke down, and Mrs Fitzherbert returned. She never actually lived in the Pavilion however, although she presided over everything that went on there. For respectability's sake (since their marriage was a secret) she had her own house on the Steine.

Meanwhile the Pavilion continued to change and grow. Bits were added in all directions. In the early years of the nineteenth century all the main rooms were redecorated in the Chinese style. In 1805 plans were drawn up for making the outside Chinese as well, but they were never carried out. Instead, between 1803 and 1808 an enormous domed stable, with a riding school attached to it, was built next door to the Pavilion in the Indian style. The prince was delighted with the result, so in 1815 work began on two huge new rooms which were added to either end of the Pavilion. They were also in the Indian style and the rest of the main building was remodelled to go with them. This last and culminating change was

Fantasy made possible by the latest technology. The domes and minarets that make up the skyline of the Pavilion are based on a cast-iron structure. The miniature onion domes surmount a row of chimney-stacks.

26

The corridor in 1826. It joins the banqueting room to the music room, and was a general meeting place and waiting-room for the whole Pavilion.

the work of John Nash, the architect of Buckingham Palace and of the terraces round London's Regent's Park.

People at the time were fascinated by China and India. The Brighton Pavilion is much the most extraordinary result of this oriental craze, but by no means the only one. In the sixteenth century the art, architecture, and literature of Greece and Rome had been revived in Italy, and spread from there all over Europe. For two hundred years and more the 'classics' reigned supreme, and everything that was not classical was considered barbarous. Then, in the course of the eighteenth century, people became aware of other periods and other civilizations. Travel, and the great trading empires built up by the European countries, opened up the world. Historical research opened up the past. Finally, new techniques of aquatinting and lithography made it possible to produce books of splendidly coloured illustrations of buildings of all periods and countries.

Buildings in styles other than classical began to be built, at first on a small scale and rather apologetically, but then in increasing numbers. By 1800 the barriers had broken down completely. It was an exciting and liberating period, when almost anything seemed possible – in architecture as well as everything else. The Norman fantasy of Penrhyn Castle was one result, and the Chinese and Indian fantasies of the Brighton Pavilion another. China and India had all the fascination of the remote and exotic. India in particular was now closely connected to England; the exploits of Robert Clive, Warren Hastings and others had won an Indian empire, from which England derived much of its wealth.

When the last transformation of the Pavilion began, the Prince of Wales was no longer the dashing and handsome young man who had given wild parties in the 1790s. He was fat and fifty. His long relationship with Mrs Fitzherbert had broken up in 1811. Two plump mother-figures – first the Marchioness of Hertford, and then the Marchioness of Conyngham – had taken her place in his life. Owing to the madness of his father, he was the acting king of England, the Prince Regent; in 1820 his father died and he became George IV.

The Pavilion had developed into an odd combination of a holiday place by the sea and the seat of a king where councils of state were held, the conduct of the Napoleonic Wars discussed and foreign royalties entertained. It provided an escape into fantasy, but was also a palace worthy of a monarch who had taken over the sceptre from the great Mogul kings of India.

The Pavilion was never meant to be an accurate copy of Indian buildings. It used China and India as a starting-point for a building that was quite unlike anything anywhere. Bits are Chinese, bits Indian, bits Nash's own invention. The onion-shaped domes that jostle each other along the middle of the Pavilion are Indian, the two great tent-like roofs which contrast with them so beautifully to either side are, if anything, Chinese. It doesn't matter; it comes off.

The inside is just as much of a mixture, and just as successful and extraordinary. Some of the rooms are conditioned by the plan of the original Pavilion. The elegant and charming central saloon, with its domed ceiling painted to imitate a cloud-speckled sky, and panels of delicate Chinese wallpaper framed by Indian-style mouldings, is basically the saloon of 1787 redecorated. The south drawing-room (and its twin to the north) is uncomfortably low for its size because it is basically the hall and two downstairs rooms of the prince's original cottage thrown into one. The most striking rooms added by Nash were the music and banqueting rooms at either end of the Pavilion, and the long and spacious corridor or gallery that runs between them behind the saloon and the drawing-room.

The gallery was the favourite room for guests at the Pavilion to stroll about in or sit in and chat. 'Walking up and down the gallery was the favourite lounge,' one guest wrote in 1816. 'All the rooms open into this beautiful gallery, which is terminated at each end by the lightest and prettiest Chinese staircases you can imagine, made of cast iron and bamboo, with glass doors beneath, which reflect the gay lanterns, etc. at each end. There are mandarins and pagodas in abundance, plenty of sofas, Japan and China.' Guests used to assemble in the gallery before dinner and then proceed in order of rank into the banqueting room, led by the prince with the lady of highest rank on his arm.

The enormous and wonderful banqueting room is dominated by dragons. Painted dragons hiss, peer and wriggle over the gold and crimson walls. Little gold dragons hang down the blue and gold lamp standards that line the walls. A circle of six writhing silver dragons hold the huge tulip-shaped lights of the central chandelier in their mouths. The whole room is crowned by the biggest and best of the dragons. This silver and crimson monster bursts out of the forest of gigantic banana leaves that cover the domed ceiling, and holds the chain of the central chandelier in his claws.

The music room is as big and richly decorated as the banqueting room, and nearly as extraordinary. Unfortunately it was badly damaged by an incendiary a few years ago, and is still being restored. Dinners at the Pavilion tended to be followed by a concert. Even when the prince had become George IV, the highlight of the programme was often the king singing solo, accompanied by his orchestra of seventy performers or by one of his prettiest guests on the piano. His voice was not very good but was said to have 'force, gaiety, and spirit'.

The king told a guest that he cried for joy when he thought of the delights of his Pavilion. He was a product of the days when the public-school code had not yet taught the English upper classes that they shouldn't make an exhibition of themselves – and that interest in the arts was a little suspect. When he was moved or upset he burst into tears. When he was glad to see someone he hugged them – men and women. He had the gift of making whoever he was talking to think that they were the one person in the world he wanted to see. He loved seeing people

right The elegant oval shape of the saloon dates from the days when it was first constructed beneath the central dome of Holland's enlarged Pavilion. It was redecorated in 1802, and again in 1822, in the Indo-Chinese style, to match the other rooms.

left The banqueting room is one of the most extraordinary and exotic rooms in Europe. The amazing chandelier which dominates it was one of the first in the world to be fitted with gas-light, and is supported by an enormous flying dragon.

right The slender columns of cast iron that support the roof of the kitchen are disguised as palm trees, with leaves of beaten copper. The kitchen was presided over by the prince's chef Carème, who invented caramel.

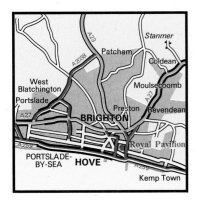

July–September (Regency Exhibition): daily 10–8. October–June: daily 10–5. Closed Christmas and Boxing Days, and three days prior to Regency Exhibition. Invalid wheelchair available upon application. Tea room open Easter–October.

enjoy themselves, whatever their class. On several occasions he gave all his servants dinner in the great kitchen at the Pavilion and 'spent a joyous hour' presiding over the meal himself.

Cast-iron and copper columns in the shape of palm trees give a touch of the East even to the kitchen. But it was also the most up-to-date and best-equipped kitchen in Europe. The fantasies of the Pavilion rested on a solid basis of the latest technology. The huge onion-shaped central dome (which contained six bedrooms for guests) is made of cast iron. So are the slender stalk-like minarets that rise between the domes. The corridor staircases are made of cast iron disguised as bamboo. The great chandeliers were originally lit by gas, for the Pavilion was almost the first building in the world to be gas-lit. The whole building was centrally heated to a temperature which most of the guests found stifling.

Everything at the Pavilion reflected the taste, character and personal choice of George IV. Queen Victoria came there a few times, but had no sympathy with the architecture and hated being stared at by the public at Brighton, which by then had grown into a large town. The Pavilion was dismantled in the 1840s and was nearly demolished. Fortunately the town of Brighton bought and preserved it. A high proportion of its contents, which had been dispersed all over the country, came back to it, many as the result of generous gifts or loans by successive kings and queens, from George V and Queen Mary onwards. From the 1920s it was gradually restored and returned to its original splendour, in which visitors can see it today.

31

Sandringham House
Norfolk

left The garden front of Sandringham, seen across one of the lakes. The wing designed by Edis in 1892 is in the foreground. 'Dear old Sandringham, the place I love better than anywhere else in the world', wrote George V.

below The saloon, through which the house is entered. It was originally used for dances, with the band up in the gallery, but when a new ballroom was built in 1885 it became the comfortable living-room it has remained to this day.

When the great red-brick mansion of Sandringham first rose amid the heaths, pinewoods, farmland and sea marshes of north Norfolk, its owner was still Prince of Wales. It was over thirty years before he succeeded his mother and became Edward VII, and in the intervening years he was often a controversial figure, and his position was a difficult one. The Sandringham estate had been bought out of his private fortune just before he came of age in 1863. His father the Prince Consort had recently died, and his mother Queen Victoria had retreated into grief and impenetrable widowhood. She worked with unremitting industry, reading all government papers and cajoling, reproving or encouraging her ministers in person or by means of a stream of letters. But she lived almost entirely at Windsor, Balmoral or Osborne and came to London as little as possible. The public very seldom saw her. After the first few years her seclusion became increasingly unpopular and was the object of much criticism.

She was, however, extremely unwilling to delegate any of her functions to her son, or even to let him know what was going on in matters of state. He was left without anything very obvious to do. Earlier Princes of Wales had tended to become actively involved in politics, and usually ended up as the focus of the opposition. But that was in the days when English kings were still ruling as well as reigning. In the course of the nineteenth century England developed into a constitutional monarchy and it became unthinkable for any member of the royal family to be seen to take political sides.

In effect, the Prince of Wales ended up by unofficially assuming what Gladstone called 'the social and visible functions of monarchy'. Unlike his mother he was constantly on view to the public. He industriously laid foundation stones, opened events, presided over banquets, and cheerfully performed all the similar chores which had become part of the duties of constitutional monarchy. But he

and his beautiful Danish wife Alexandra also became the acknowledged leaders of
Society with a capital S – a role which was still expected of the monarchy and
which Victoria had virtually ceased to fulfil.

They entered into this aspect of their life with tremendous enjoyment and
enthusiasm. They were young, handsome and full of vitality and high spirits.
They entertained lavishly, both at Sandringham and their London home
Marlborough House. They lived in a constant social whirl of parties, theatres and
balls. The prince indulged to the full his enthusiasm for racing, yachting, shooting
and pretty women. All this made them extremely popular in society, especially
the more social and political end of it. The working classes enjoyed seeing a gay
and glamorous couple living the kind of life they felt that they would lead if they
could afford it. But the middle classes were more critical.

The Victorian middle classes tended to be serious-minded and censorious. They
were often shocked by the extravagance, gaiety, lack of intellectual interests and
easy-going morality of the set over which the prince and princess presided. It was
true that the upper classes of the time were very careful to keep up a decorous
façade; but occasionally something happened which exposed behaviour
unacceptable to the nonconformist conscience. The prince was called as a
material witness to a divorce case in 1870 and was involved in a baccarat scandal in
1891. In both cases he had played an innocent part; but many people felt that he
should not be moving in circles where that kind of thing could happen.

Criticism concentrated on the prince's behaviour in London and abroad;
Sandringham was the least controversial aspect of his life. He went there to rest
from London and to live the traditional life of a prosperous country gentleman,
shooting, farming, entertaining his friends and neighbours and looking after his

Victorian masculinity triumphant. Edward VII when Prince of Wales presiding over a shooting party at Sandringham in 1867. He is surrounded by his friends, including Christopher Sykes who became a favourite victim of the prince's weakness for practical jokes.

tenantry. It was something new for a Prince and Princess of Wales to live in this way; it was very different from the Prince Regent's hot-house existence in Brighton Pavilion. Both Edward and Alexandra fulfilled the role to perfection. 'What a blessing it would be', commented a newspaper of the time, 'if we could Sandringhamize Marlborough House, and establish in St James's Park something of the sense of the obligations of responsibility and of the conscious, intimate relationship to the poor which exists on the Norfolk estate. There is a general concurrence of opinion that as a landlord, as an agriculturist and as a country gentleman, the Prince sets an example which might be followed with advantage throughout the country.'

Of course Sandringham is no longer exactly as it was when Edward VII died in 1910 and Queen Alexandra in 1925. Subsequent kings and queens have all made changes. There have been many alterations in the gardens, and the dark paint and lavish clutter in which the Edwardians delighted have been replaced by lighter colours and less crowded rooms. But the personalities and tastes of King Edward and Queen Alexandra are still very much in evidence there, especially in those parts of the house and grounds which are open to the public.

No one could pretend that Sandringham is architecturally distinguished. Neither the prince nor the princess were very discriminating in visual matters. What they wanted was a large, comfortable, hospitable house in which they could put up a great many people. It was, and still is, a country house rather than a palace. There are no throne rooms, council chambers or splendid state rooms. As Prince of Wales, Edward VII had no need for them; and even when he succeeded as king, he used Sandringham as a place in which to escape from palace protocol and live, as far as he was able, the life of a private individual. Subsequent monarchs have followed his example.

When the estate was first bought in 1862 it centred round a house which was neither very large nor very interesting. This was almost entirely rebuilt in 1869–70 to the designs of A.J.Humbert, and a ballroom was added in 1885. The house was much enlarged in 1892 after it had been badly damaged by fire. Humbert was an architect much employed by the Victorian royal family, for no very good reason. The ballroom and the additions of 1892 were by Colonel R.W.Edis, a much abler designer. He was not a serious military man; he was a professional architect who in his spare time became commanding officer of the Artists' Rifles – a job which he took over from the great Victorian Royal Academician Lord Leighton.

Humbert used a rather ugly combination of red brick and yellowish Bath stone for the walls and gabled roofs of the main building. Architecturally the most attractive part of the house is the long wing to the east which was added after the fire of 1891 by Colonel Edis. It joins on to the billiard room, which was originally the conservatory and was the only part of the old house to survive the first rebuilding. Edis's wing is built of an extremely attractive combination of red brick and the local carstone, which is a rich orange-brown. Its delicate scale and charming colour make an agreeable contrast to Humbert's neo-Jacobean mansion.

Edward VII was a loyal and devoted friend who adored fun and company but lacked the resources to keep him contented on his own. The life of a big house-party suited him to perfection. He was an admirable host. House-parties at Sandringham were gay, comfortable and not at all formal. Life centred round the big entrance hall known as the saloon, which was (and still is) furnished as a comfortable general sitting-room. Originally it was also used as a ballroom with the band up in the minstrel's gallery over the entrance; but this function was transferred to the new ballroom (which is not open to the public) in the 1890s. Beyond the saloon the small drawing-room, the large drawing-room and the dining-room run into each other, and all look out over the garden. The large drawing-room is presided over by a full-length portrait of Queen Alexandra; and

right Prince George of Wales, later George V, and his elder brother the Duke of Clarence, painted when they were both serving as midshipmen. The duke (on the left), who was something of a problem child, died of pneumonia at Sandringham in 1892. His succession to the throne and his fiancée, later Queen Mary, both passed to his younger brother.

left The drawing-room, which looks out over the garden. Late Victorian furniture and decoration are combined with Chinese ornaments and other objects, many of them collected by Queen Mary.

April–September: Tuesday–Thursday 11–4.45. May–August: Monday–Thursday 11–4.45, Sunday 12–4.45. *House* closed mid-July–early August each year, *Grounds* closed during last week of July.

although many of the objects, especially the Chinese jade and crystal in the show-cases, were collected by Queen Mary, the room is still evocative of the elegance of Queen Alexandra herself and the great Edwardian ladies who congregated round her. The male room at Sandringham, as in other great houses of its period, was the billiard room (not shown to visitors) beyond the dining-room. There used to be a bowling-alley beyond this, looked after by an African servant whom the prince brought back from a trip to Egypt. The billiard room and dining-room are connected to the ballroom by a long corridor, filled today with an evocative collection of royal portraits and mementoes and a splendid series of late Victorian and Edwardian bronzes.

The sporting pictures and cases of game on show in the corridor bear witness to what has always been one of the great features of Sandringham life. Late Victorian country houses were famous for their huge and splendidly organized shoots, none more so than Sandringham. In Edward VII's day the army of beaters wore a special uniform – blue blouses, black chimney-pot hats with a red ribbon, and a red badge and individual badge for each beater. Operations were controlled by the mounted head keeper, in a black billycock hat, red sash and green velveteen outfit.

These uniforms are sometimes on show in the museum which has been formed in what used to be the coach-house and in other outbuildings. Its contents include big-game trophies, racing relics and trophies, vintage royal cars, a vintage fire-engine and other mementoes of the Sandringham Estate Fire Brigade. A further great attraction of Sandringham is the magnificently planted and beautifully kept grounds. Queen Alexandra's favourite dogs are buried under touching little tombstones in one corner of them. Another evocative reminder of the queen is the little summer-house overlooking one of the string of lakes created by Edward VII when Prince of Wales. An inscription inside it reads: 'The Queen's Nest – a small offering to The Blessed Lady from Her Beloved Majesty's very devoted old servant General Probyn, 1913.' It is redolent of the chivalrous devotion which King Edward, Queen Alexandra and subsequent members of the royal family have inspired in those who served under them.

2 FAMILY HOMES

Penshurst Place
Kent

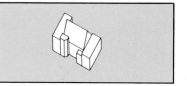

a

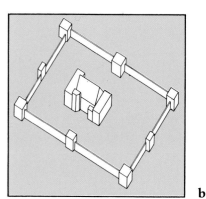

b

Some country houses rise completely formed out of virgin soil, or phoenix-like out of the ashes of an old building. They are the perfect product of a few years; and any subsequent alterations seem like a blot on the original design. Hardwick is an obvious example of this kind of house; but other houses grow gradually over many centuries. They give a feeling of slow growth, of tradition, of generation after generation living there and adapting the house to fit its needs. Few country houses give this feeling more strongly than Penshurst.

Its growth has been so gradual and complicated that working out its history in detail presents an almost insoluble problem. There is general agreement about the main lines; but much remains to be discovered – and probably never will be discovered. The average visitor may be happy enough to enjoy his ignorance – to wander round the rooms, look through windows at ranges of buildings running out in unexpected directions, observe the curious way in which stone changes into brick or brick is patched with stone, and leave it to others to try to explain how it all happened.

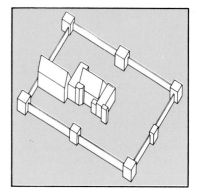

c

On the whole, Penshurst is fascinating because of its overall effect, not because of the splendour or beauty of its individual bits. But there is one exception. The great hall is one of the most exciting buildings in the country. It is enormous, ancient, powerful and beautiful. It is built of the local stone, which is one of the loveliest in England – a rich golden yellow streaked with reddish brown. Great arches scoop into its massive walls, and solid buttresses strengthen them; but under the arches are windows of delicate and lace-like tracery. Inside, it is a vast and cavernous space, with a weathered and uneven floor of ancient tiles. High above, crouching wooden figures, mysteriously truncated below the knees, support the arched timbers of the roof. No more satisfying way of covering a great space has been discovered than the timber roofs of medieval England. The roof at Penshurst may be the work of the king's master carpenter John Hurley; and it is worthy of a king.

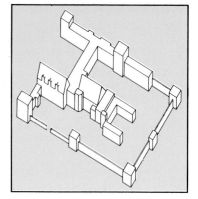

d

It was not built for a king however. The hall is probably the oldest part of Penshurst, and was built in about 1341 for Sir John de Pulteney. Pulteney was a remarkable man. In the fourteenth century great houses and castles were almost invariably built by the king or the royal family, or by powerful nobles who

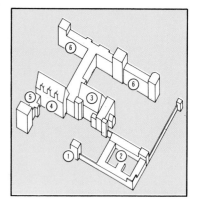

e

Key to diagrams

from the top
a. The original Penshurst Hall and cross wings, c.1340.
b. Penshurst as encircled with walls and towers, c.1390.
c. The hall block extended, probably by the Duke of Bedford, c.1430.
d. Penshurst as enlarged by the Sidneys in the sixteenth and seventeenth centuries. The house is extended out to and along the walls; the fortifications begin to crumble.
e. Penshurst today. 1. The king's tower. 2. The nineteenth-century stables. 3. The great hall. 4. The state rooms. 5. The long gallery. 6. The family wing. The king's tower is virtually all that remains of the original fortifications.

right The fourteenth-century great hall. Food came up from the kitchen through the doors beyond the screen, and the hall was heated by an open fire in the middle of the floor.

far left The exterior of the hall and the king's tower.

preceding pages Penshurst seen across the garden from the south.

gained their reputations fighting for the king (or sometimes for themselves). But Pulteney was one of the first of a long line of English merchants who made their money trading in the city and then invested it in the country. Not only was he one of the first, he was one of the most successful. He operated on the same kind of scale as the Medici in Italy in the fifteenth century or the Rothschilds in Europe in the nineteenth. He was both a money-lender and a wool-merchant on an enormous scale. He financed the king and much of the Hundred Years War. The hall at Penshurst shows how well he did for himself; at the time it was one of the biggest in England, and it still is. But the Black Death, which wiped out perhaps one third of the population of England, wiped out Pulteney among them in 1349.

His house at Penshurst was never meant to be a castle, but some time after his death – probably at the end of the fourteenth century – it was given enough in the way of fortification to turn it into a fortified manor-house. It may have been that its then owner Sir John Devereux had been worried by the Peasants' Revolt in 1381 and wanted walls and towers that would keep peasants at bay. The way it was fortified was unusual in that it was completely symmetrical – something hard to envisage in view of the almost chaotic irregularity of Penshurst today. Pulteney's hall and the buildings attached to it were made the detached centre of a

41

huge walled enclosure. The enclosure took the form of a rectangle punctuated by eight towers, one at each corner and one in the middle of each side.

These towers acted as magnets to future generations. Ranges of new buildings began to be built out from the centre towards them. Sometimes they got as far as the towers, sometimes they didn't. Some of the towers and most of the intervening walls were later demolished, leaving the confused pattern of building which is there today.

Roughly speaking, the building grew in two main directions. One direction provided rooms for the family and the other rooms for state. It is the state rooms which the public see today; the family are still living in the family rooms.

The state rooms spread out from the hall in two jumps. In about 1430 Penshurst was bought by the Duke of Bedford. He was a royal duke, the third son of Henry IV. While his nephew Henry VI was still a minor, he acted as Regent of England – and of those parts of France which England then controlled. It was probably he who built a grand new building on to one corner of Pulteney's block in the 1430s. Its main purpose was to contain an enormous room in which the duke could, if necessary, entertain his royal nephew in state. For between Pulteney's time and his an important change had taken place in the life of great people in England. One really *can* envisage Pulteney seated at the centre of a 'high table', raised up at one end of the hall at Penshurst, surveying his household eating at long tables down below him. It would have been a crowded scene, for the household of someone as rich as Pulteney was likely to consist of a hundred to two hundred people. The big room beyond the hall, up the stone stairs that lead out of it, was just for Pulteney to retire and sleep in. But around 1400 great people began to remove from the hall and eat in another room, separate from the main bulk of their household.

The inside of Bedford's building has been completely altered. The next addition to the state rooms survives relatively untouched. In the late sixteenth or early seventeenth century one of the corner towers was joined to Bedford's building in order to make a long gallery on the first floor. The gallery is still there, complete with its delicate chestnut-brown panelling. The furniture is arranged along the walls with the centre left clear. It gives a good idea of how these galleries were used – to pace up and down for exercise on a wet or cold day.

Hanging along the walls of the gallery are the portraits of the Sidney family, who had become the owners of Penshurst in 1552. From the Duke of Bedford the

below left Splendid furniture of the seventeenth and eighteenth centuries in Queen Elizabeth's room. It is one of the state rooms carved out of a medieval room where the Dukes of Bedford and Buckingham used to feast.

house had passed to the Duke of Gloucester, and from the Duke of Gloucester to the Dukes of Buckingham. The third Duke of Buckingham was beheaded in 1521; his only crime seems to have been that he was too rich. Henry VIII took over his houses and property, including Penshurst. In 1552 Edward VI gave Penshurst to Sir William Sidney who had been his tutor and had become the steward of his household. It has belonged to his descendants ever since.

The Sidneys occupy a very special place in English history. They were not an old family. They were one of a small group of families whom the Tudors raised to power and made their inner circle of ministers and advisers. The Dudleys, Herberts, Greys and Cecils were also in the circle, but the Sidneys stood a little apart from the others. This was partly because they were unusually intelligent and well educated, were writers themselves and discriminating and generous patrons of other writers and men of learning; but this could also be said of others in the circle. The distinctive quality of the Sidneys was that they were unusually honest.

Most successful Elizabethans were unashamedly on the make. They did as well as they possibly could out of bribes, jobs, perquisites and fiddles. They aimed to make a great deal of money, and often succeeded. Sir Henry Sidney, the son of the Sir William who was granted Penshurst, was in a different class. He served Elizabeth faithfully for many years, mostly as Lord President of Wales and Lord Lieutenant of Ireland. He won a reputation for just and generous rule; and he lost rather than made money.

His famous son Philip never actually owned Penshurst because he died before his father. He was equally high-principled, but a much more dazzling personality. He was 'the most accomplished cavalier of his time'. Strikingly handsome, brave, a poet and a patron of poets, he was killed when he was only thirty-two, fighting at the Battle of Zutphen in Holland. His last act, of giving his water-bottle to another dying soldier, has become legendary.

The fact that the Sidneys never made large profits out of their various posts does much to explain Penshurst. They built a good deal of what is there today, including the long gallery wing and much of the private wing. But nothing they did was elaborate, and they altered or added to the existing buildings instead of replacing them.

In about 1612 Ben Jonson wrote a poem about Penshurst. He may have been inspired partly by pique; he had been insulted (or so he thought) when dining

below A green velvet four-poster bed dating from the time of William III in a room below the long gallery.

below right The long gallery. It was built in the early seventeenth century to join the main block of the house to the south-west tower, and is lined with portraits of the Sidney family.

with Robert Cecil at Theobalds. His poem contrasts the life-style and buildings of the Cecils at Theobalds and Hatfield with those of the Sidneys at Penshurst, very unfavourably to the former. But the result is a moving and beautiful description of a way of life and building, which did much to establish Englishmen's vision of the ideal country house life. Jonson describes a household rooted in the neighbourhood, living abundantly but not ostentatiously on food grown on its own lands, and dispensing generous but unpatronizing hospitality to local people of every kind. As for the house itself:

> Thou art not, Penshurst, built to envious show
> Of touch or marble; nor canst boast a row
> Of polished pillars, or a roof of gold.
> Thou hast no lantern, whereof tales are told,
> Or stair, or courts; but stand'st an ancient pile,
> And these grudged at, art reverenced the while.

Philip Sidney's younger brother Robert was created Earl of Leicester in 1618. The last Earl of Leicester died in 1743, and Penshurst went by way of daughters to the Perry and Shelley families, both of whom changed their name to Sidney. In the late eighteenth century the house passed through a bad patch and emerged in decay and semi-derelict. Much of what one sees today is the result of slow and conservative restoration, starting in the mid-nineteenth century and going on until the present day. The gardens date from this period, and are exceptionally tranquil and beautiful. Most of the state rooms were restored and redecorated in the mid-nineteenth century; but their contents are almost all of the sixteenth, seventeenth and eighteenth centuries. They include much beautiful late seventeenth- and eighteenth-century furniture, and a fascinating series of family portraits. The Sidneys seem to have had an especial fondness for being painted in groups. Robert Sidney's demure and pop-eyed daughters contrast delightfully with the arch and frolicsome daughters of fat William Perry, who married the Sidney heiress. One's only complaint is that no surviving portrait does justice either to the looks or character of Philip Sidney, 'the most accomplished cavalier of his time'.

above left Barbara Sidney, later Countess of Leicester, and her children, painted in 1596. Her son and heir wears a sword and carries a feathered cap to show his importance.

above William Perry, his wife Elizabeth Sidney and their children, painted in the mid-eighteenth century.

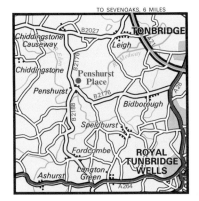

April–September: *Grounds* daily (except Monday and Friday) 11.30–6; *House* daily (except Monday and Friday) 2–6, Bank Holidays 11.30–6. Refreshments available.

Hatfield House
Hertfordshire

Hatfield House
Hertfordshire

Great English families follow a number of different patterns. Some are founded by an ancestor who makes a name and a fortune, and then relapse into comfortable somnolence and never do anything noteworthy again. Some, having been obscure country gentry for generations, suddenly produce a famous man. A few keep up a high level of achievement over an impressively long period.

The Cecils have their own pattern. For two generations William Cecil, who became Lord Burghley, and his son Robert Cecil, later Earl of Salisbury, were successively the most powerful men in England. Lord Burghley, from relatively humble origins, rose to be Lord Treasurer and the chief minister, friend and trusted adviser of Queen Elizabeth. Robert Cecil took over his position in Queen Elizabeth's old age. He continued it under James I, whose peaceful succession to the throne of England he engineered.

Then for nearly two hundred years the Cecils of Hatfield went into a steady decline. By the end of the eighteenth century the house was in decay and the sixth earl had married his steward's daughter, taken to drink and low company and sold the silver. But three generations later the third Marquess (and ninth Earl) of Salisbury was both rich and famous. He was prime minister for nearly seventeen years, and Queen Victoria was almost as dependent on him as Queen Elizabeth on his famous ancestor; many of his children and grandchildren were to turn out brilliant or distinguished. The Cecils had staged a comeback.

The two periods of brilliance and the twilight in between are accurately reflected in Hatfield as it exists today. The first period produced the house; but although its main structure and much of its decoration survive relatively unaltered its surroundings, its gardens, its atmosphere and many of its contents are redolent of the second. The space in between has left little mark on the house, apart from a few portraits and pieces of furniture.

Robert Cecil, the first Earl of Salisbury, was only Lord Burghley's second son. Most of his father's great properties went to his elder brother who became Earl of Exeter; his descendants still live at Burghley House, near Stamford. Robert Cecil inherited a certain amount of land and Theobalds House, a few miles away from Hatfield. Theobalds had been Lord Burghley's main residence; and Queen Elizabeth, who liked living at her subjects' expense, had spent so much time there that it had become almost an alternative palace. To make it big enough for the queen and her court, Burghley had enlarged it to enormous size; it was not so very much smaller than Hampton Court. Robert Cecil continued to entertain Elizabeth, and later James I, at Theobalds. But the expense of maintaining it was crippling even for someone as high in royal favour as Cecil. It may have been rather a relief to him when James – who had fallen in love with Theobalds and was not so careful with his money as Elizabeth – suggested that Theobalds should become royal property, in exchange for a generous grant of crown lands. The grant would include Hatfield and the royal palace which stood on it. This was a sizeable Tudor building dating from the late fifteenth century. It had been lived in by Queen Elizabeth when she was still a princess, kept as a semi-prisoner and regarded with considerable suspicion by her half-sister Mary; it was there that she heard that Mary had died and she had become Queen of England. But neither Elizabeth, after her accession, nor James I, after his, had taken much interest in it.

Cecil (by now Earl of Salisbury) agreed to the exchange, which took place in 1607. However, he was not the sort of person to content himself with a building a hundred and thirty years old; he wanted something in the latest fashion. Almost

The north front. The surviving portion of the Tudor bishop's palace, which Hatfield House superseded, is down the hill to the right. Sir Robert Cecil, later Earl of Salisbury, deliberately chose a new site on the crest of a hill, so that his splendid new house could be seen and admired from all over the surrounding countryside.

preceding page The former main entrance on the south front of Hatfield House.

46

as soon as he acquired the property he began to build. He chose a new site, farther up the hill than the old palace; from it the ground sloped away on three sides so that the new building, unlike the old one, dominated the neighbourhood.

The new Hatfield was not nearly as large as Theobalds, but it was very far from small. Cecil built it in the anticipation that James I and his queen, Anne of Denmark, would be regular visitors. The house was divided into two main blocks, to east and west, each containing a royal apartment on the first floor, one for the king and one for the queen. The two blocks were joined by a central building, forming the stroke of the letter H. On the first floor this contained a splendid long gallery, joining king's apartment to queen's apartment. On the ground floor was a great hall, rising through two storeys, with staircases to either side of it leading up to the two royal apartments. On the floor below the king's rooms Cecil made a less grand but still very handsome set of rooms for his own everyday use.

The house rose at amazing speed. Everything was done with the utmost lavishness. Marble was brought from Italy, trees and plants imported from the continent. The house glittered with colour inside and out; all the many domes

and turrets were finished off with gold leaf, so that the whole house flashed and glittered from a distance. The expense was enormous; but politicians in those days expected to make money out of their careers, and took as their right the kind of perquisites which would cause a major political scandal today. Salisbury, as the most powerful politician of all, made more money than anyone. He had not only to pay for the house, however, but also to acquire enough land and property to enable his descendants to maintain it and live in a style suitable to their position. This needed time; and time, as it turned out, was what he did not have.

Salisbury had been born slightly deformed, with a humped back about which he was desperately sensitive. He was never strong, and he worked fantastically hard. He died in 1612, aged only forty-nine. His house was only just finished and he probably never had time to move into it. Moreover, it was still unpaid for at his death, and the debt had to be paid off by selling some of his carefully acquired land. His descendants were still very rich, but not as rich as he had hoped for. This, combined with the failure of subsequent earls to do well in politics, the excessive generosity of the third earl to his younger children, and the extravagance of the fourth earl, all contributed to the family's decline.

Today the outside of Hatfield is much as the first earl left it, except that some of the turrets and all the colouring and gilding with which it originally blazed have disappeared. Visitors' first impressions, too are misleading. The house was designed to be entered by the south front, which is rich with stonework and carving; today one comes in by what was originally the back door on the north. Impressive though the north front is in its rather gaunt simplicity, Salisbury never intended that it should figure so prominently.

Inside, too, much remains of the original decoration, although almost all the original furnishings have disappeared, with the exception of some splendid Elizabethan and Jacobean portraits. But the hall is still rich with Jacobean plasterwork and carving. Strange grotesque figures support the great beams that cross the ceiling. The heavily decorated gallery running across the far end (its

The long gallery was originally planned to join the two separate state apartments. By the nineteenth century it was being used as an occasional ballroom, or as a sitting-room for the huge house-parties for which Hatfield became famous.

right The wife of the first Marquess of Salisbury, painted by Reynolds. Her dash and determination rescued Hatfield from a long period of decline.

The main staircase originally glittered with painting and gilding, and was one of the first and most famous of the carved wooden staircases which became fashionable under James I. The gate was to keep dogs from going upstairs.

elaborate screen makes it look rather like something in a harem) is often described as a musicians' gallery; and Salisbury certainly had a delicate ear for music, and his own choir of trained boys. But the gallery may also have been planned as a kind of state box, from which Salisbury or the king could watch plays and masques when they were put on in the hall – as often happened in Jacobean times.

By the time Hatfield was built neither family nor guests ate any longer in the halls of great houses. At Hatfield informal meals would have been eaten in the parlour on the ground floor, and grand meals in one of the two great chambers in the king's and queen's apartments. The great staircase at the far end of the hall was especially grand because it led up to the king's great chamber. It was and still is covered with delicate carving; bulging cherubs hold up musical instruments on every alternate post. Everything was originally gay with gilding and colour. When it was built the staircase was a fashion-setting novelty, for wooden staircases cantilevered out round an open well had only just been invented. The carpenter who made it, Robert Lyminge, was so important that he seems to have been consulted about the design of the whole house; no architect in the modern sense was employed at all.

The king's great chamber is now known as King James's drawing-room. A life-size bronze statue of the king, placed there when the house was built, surveys the room from the great Jacobean chimney-piece, but the room is otherwise

left The marble hall. In Jacobean days it was probably used for occasional banquets, plays and entertainments, and as a dining hall for servants.

below King James's drawing-room. The statue of the king over the fireplace surveys what was designed mainly as a state dining-room for royal visits. It became a drawing-room in the eighteenth century.

much changed since James's day. Perhaps the only original furnishing from it to have survived is the great painted organ, now downstairs in the armoury. This was originally brought from Holland for the great chamber and not, curiously enough, for the chapel.

The chapel at Hatfield is much less altered than King James's drawing-room. It retains its original stained glass, painted decoration and elaborate gallery, from which royalty and nobility used to attend services while the rest of the household worshipped down below. But the most complete and attractive of the Jacobean rooms at Hatfield is the long gallery. It is lined from floor to richly plastered and gilded ceiling with original panelling; it is a stately room and yet at the same time an intimate one – with Queen Elizabeth's silk stockings on show at one end of it.

King James in the drawing-room looks across today at Reynolds's superb portrait of the first marchioness, who reigned at Hatfield for fifty years from 1773. Reynolds has shown her as she was, dashing and imperious. Essentially, it was she who saved Hatfield. She was a loud-mouthed arrogant Irishwoman, addicted to gambling, hunting and bad language; but she had endless determination and guts. By lavish entertaining, stylish living, and refurnishing and redecorating much of the house, she put Hatfield on the map again. It was due more to her than to her well-meaning husband that Hatfield became the centre of the Tory party, then making a comeback after long years of being overshadowed by the Whigs – and that her husband was made a marquess. And she had a hand in another event that was to be extremely important for Hatfield. In 1821 her eldest

right Unlike many aristocrats
the later Cecils were a reading
rather than a sporting family,
and the library's pleasantly
book-lined walls were meant
for serious use. The portrait is
of Robert Cecil, Earl of
Salisbury, the builder of
Hatfield; it was made of
mosaic in Venice.

son married Frances Mary Gascoyne. She was an intelligent, serious-minded girl
and also a great heiress (for which reason the nineteenth-century Cecils became
Gascoyne-Cecils). At last there was enough money to support Hatfield in style.

The marchioness used to ride round the estate scattering guineas to the poor
from a velvet bag held by a groom. She lived on to a gallant old age, made-up to
the nines, dressed like a young girl, still hunting, gambling and playing cards deep
into the night, and embarrassing her family by her debts and her refusal to grow
old gracefully. She went out in style, although rather horribly. In 1835 she was
burned to death in the west wing at Hatfield (the feathers in her hair-do may have
caught fire from a candle) and the whole west wing was gutted with her.

Endowed with the first marchioness's force of character, and the second
marchioness's intelligence and money, the Cecils sailed into their Victorian and
Edwardian heyday. Hatfield became one of the most famous houses in England.
Balls and garden-parties were held in profusion. Victoria and Albert came to stay;
so did the Shah of Persia and both Disraeli *and* Gladstone. Huge house-parties
were given there constantly. To have six guests staying in addition to the family
was called 'having no one in the house'. Meals were eaten in the great hall in
summer and in a new upstairs dining-room in winter; sofas and armchairs spilled
all down the long gallery; high politics were discussed in the library. So was
almost everything else. The prime minister, his wife and seven children (and later
his grandchildren) were like nobody else, but very much like each other. They
were lively, argumentative, absent-minded, untidy and full of fun and ideas,

End March–early October: *House and West Gardens* Tuesday–Saturday 12–5, Sunday 2–5.30, Bank Holidays 11–5. No dogs in house. *Park* daily 10.30–8. Closed Good Friday. Restaurant.

which they expressed in a curious staccato voice peculiar to the family. Children were expected to join in the conversation and have their own opinions.

The Victorian Cecils were not sensitive to beauty. There are some country houses, like Uppark, where generation after generation had the gift of buying pretty things and creating harmonious interiors. The nineteenth-century Cecils lacked this gift entirely (and probably didn't want it). Many alterations were made at Hatfield in this period; perhaps none of them were actively ugly, but on the other hand none were very sympathetic.

The one exception was the gardens (the original Jacobean gardens had vanished entirely) and even these owe much to later and less philistine generations. The beautiful east gardens are not open to the public, but the west gardens are. When visiting them it is worth walking up far enough to get a glimpse of the south front. This was Robert Cecil's entrance front, and is not otherwise accessible to visitors. Even here the prime minister's lack of interest in how things looked is in evidence. Asphalt paths, as in a municipal garden, run through the woods. The prime minister, when old and overweight, had them laid so that he could ride through the grounds on a tricycle. In a broad-brimmed hat and a cloak he would puff slowly along, with a child or footman there to push him when he got stuck.

Traquair House
Peeblesshire

Traquair House
Peeblesshire

The first thing that strikes an English visitor to Traquair is how completely unlike it is to an English house. This is not always true of Scottish country houses, but it is true of many of those which date (or mostly date) from the sixteenth and seventeenth centuries; and nowhere more so than Traquair. If it is reminiscent of country houses anywhere else, it is of *châteaux* in France.

Driving along quiet country roads in France one quite often finds oneself looking through wrought-iron gates and up an avenue of trees at a peaceful *château* with a high, time-stained façade ending in a steep roof and a sprinkling of little turrets – as at Traquair. The resemblance is not entirely accidental. France and Scotland in the sixteenth century had more ties with each other than England and Scotland. Mary Queen of Scots, who has many links with Traquair, had a French mother and for a time was queen of France as well as of Scotland. Even in the eighteenth century the Earls of Traquair sent their daughters to be educated in French convents in Paris. This was because they were Catholics and Jacobites, and in England and Scotland Catholic schools were still illegal.

Its Catholic and Jacobite tradition is vital to the history of Traquair. It meant that for nearly two hundred years the family belonged to a minority which, when it was not being actively persecuted, was heavily taxed and not allowed to take part in public life. As a result there was never much money at Traquair – enough to make minor alterations, and add a room or two here and there, but never to do more than that. Traquair slipped into a backwater and acquired the mysterious feeling that it still has of being a house where time has stood still.

Even before the days of persecution Traquair had not been a rich house. The family had its period of splendour, but it only lasted ten years or so, during which the Stuarts of Traquair acquired their earldom. Unlike so many other country houses it was never rebuilt or remodelled. It grew bit by bit, a little on top and a little to one side, so gently and all of a piece that it is often hard to distinguish the work of one generation from that of another.

The main front of the house faces west, so that it lights up peacefully in the evening sun, beyond the long shadows thrown by the trees of the avenue. Concealed in its left-hand end is an old tower with walls many feet thick. Parts of this may date back to the twelfth century, when Traquair belonged to the kings of Scotland. In the fifteenth century James III of Scotland gave it to William Rogers, his master of music. In 1478 Rogers sold it to the king's uncle the Earl of Buchan, who gave it to his son James Stuart. The present Maxwell Stuarts of Traquair descend from him, and the twentieth laird lives there today with his family.

The Stuarts of Traquair were loyal servants to their royal kinsmen in good times and in bad. James, the first laird, was killed with James IV at the battle of Flodden Field. The fourth laird John Stuart was knighted by Mary Queen of Scots, who made him captain of her guard. In 1565, after the murder of her musician and favourite David Rizzio he organized her midnight escape from Holyrood Palace to Dunbar. In 1566 she and her husband Henry Darnley stayed at Traquair on a hunting expedition. The fifth laird Sir William Stuart was high in the favour of Mary's son James VI of Scotland and I of England.

All this time Traquair was growing bit by bit, but the result was quite unlike the contemporary Elizabethan and Jacobean houses of England. The Scots had colder winters and less money than the English. Glass was an expensive luxury. Traquair, like other Scottish houses of its period, has relatively tiny windows burrowed through the thick walls. On the outside almost the only decoration is

preceding page The entrance front of Traquair House, which looks over the forecourt down a long avenue. Like a natural growth Traquair spread upwards and outwards over several hundred years, assuming its final form in the late seventeenth century.

above From the east the house rises high and romantic over the water-meadows along the River Tweed. A riverside terrace joins two little domed summer-houses, built in the late seventeenth century, and decorated with paintings of gods and goddesses.

on the top floor. Here the pedimented dormer windows in the steep roof and the little corner turrets show the influence of France.

Much of the top floor was built on in the 1640s by John Stuart, the seventh laird and first Earl of Traquair. His additions left the main part of the house looking very much as it does today. This earl was the best-known and most controversial of the owners of Traquair. Charles I made him an earl in 1633, when he was only thirty-three. In 1636 he was made Lord High Treasurer of Scotland and became its virtual ruler, under the king. The earl seemed all set for a long and successful career, which would probably have involved the rebuilding of his house in the latest fashion, but the furious opposition of many people in Scotland to the king's religious policy, and the Civil War which followed it, shipwrecked him. He was dismissed from the treasurership in 1641, and was kept prisoner in England from

1648 to 1652. He died in poverty in 1659. It was said that he 'wanted bread before he died' and that 'he had nought to pay for cobbling his boots'.

The earl had been a Protestant. His son married two Catholic wives in succession, and the family have been Catholics ever since. The troubles of Traquair were well under way. To say or hear mass was illegal. At Traquair it was celebrated in secret in a small room at the top of the house, until, in the more tolerant nineteenth century, a chapel was made in one of the wings. This top room had a view of the approach roads; the house was frequently searched by the authorities, and if a search-party was seen coming the priest could escape down a little staircase concealed behind a cupboard in a corner of the room.

In 1688, when the 'Glorious Revolution' which brought William III to England had raised religious feeling to boiling point, a Protestant mob came out from Peebles, ran through the house and destroyed all the religious objects they found there. A list of these 'Popish Trinkets' is one of the documents on show at Traquair. From then on the family were in double trouble – as Catholics *and* Jacobites. Their feelings are demonstrated by an engraved glass at Traquair:

> God bless the Prince of Wales
> The true-born Prince of Wales,
> Sent us by thee
> Send him soon over
> And kick out Hanover
> And soon we'll recover
> Our old libertie.

Traquair became one of the main Jacobite centres in the south of Scotland. At the time of the 1715 Rising the fourth earl was imprisoned in Edinburgh Castle as a Jacobite sympathizer. The fifth earl spent two years in the Tower of London for his part in the 1745 Rising, accompanied by his devoted wife who refused to be separated from him. One of the most famous traditions or legends of Traquair is

left The library, up on the
second floor, was decorated
and fitted out in the mid-
eighteenth century, and has
scarcely been touched since.
Even the books remain where
they were arranged in the
shelves over two hundred years
ago.

right The bed in the king's
room was remodelled in the
early eighteenth century, but is
said to be based on one slept in
by Mary Queen of Scots.

below A mid-seventeenth-
century harpsichord, panelling
of a few decades later and
painted decoration of the 1750s
merge with family portraits
and old furniture in the high
drawing-room.

that he entertained Bonny Prince Charlie there, and as he sped him on his way he closed the great gates at the end of the avenue behind him and vowed that they would never be opened again until a Stuart king was crowned in London.

In the intervals of their troubles, however, the earls continued to add and alter at Traquair. The most work was done by the fourth earl, although lack of money kept him from doing as much as he would have liked. At the end of the seventeenth century the architect James Smith produced plans for rebuilding much of the entrance front to make it symmetrical; but in the end the earl contented himself with less ambitious alterations. Even so, what he did gives the house much of its character. He planted the long avenue, and added two wings and wrought-iron railings to make a forecourt and give an air of formality to the entrance front of the house. On the other side he built a terrace, ending in two little domed pavilions. These each have a panelled room with a painted ceiling; one has just been restored and was opened to the public in 1978. Inside the house he panelled the more important rooms, including the 'high drawing-room', with the ante-room and king's bedchamber beyond it.

The high drawing-room is so called not because it is a high room but because it is on the first floor. Early Scottish houses often had their main rooms on the first or even second floor, and this practice continued well into the eighteenth century, but changing fashions and a more secure way of life gradually brought them down to the ground floor. At Traquair there is a room (now the museum room) on the second floor that is as large as the high drawing-room. By the beginning of the eighteenth century this had fallen into disuse; and at the end of the eighteenth century a new drawing-room and dining-room were made at ground level in one of the wings.

Before then more alterations had been made by the fifth earl, probably after the troubles of 1745 and his two years in prison which followed them. He brought in an unidentified artist to give an extra touch of individuality to the panelled rooms by painting the panels over their doors and fireplaces. A downstairs room has two shelves of painted books partly concealed by a painted curtain. Over the fireplace in the high drawing-room ships in harbour are framed by pretty rococo scrolls painted in gold, with gilded trophies of fruit and arms over the doorways. The most individual work of this period, however, is the library on the second floor. This is a delightful place in which to read in peace, secure from interruption. The

walls are lined from floor to ceiling with old books. The cove which runs round the room is painted with heads of classical writers and philosophers. In addition to being very decorative, these serve as a reference system. 'Horace 2 XII', for instance, gives the book stack, shelf number, and position of the book on the shelf. The books were all catalogued on this system in a great leather-bound volume when the library was installed. The system still works today for the books are all in their original positions.

All these rooms at Traquair have a very special character. None of them is elaborately decorated, because there was never enough money – certainly not enough to order everything of the best up from London, as at Blair Castle. The rooms have low ceilings and small windows yet they are not dark or depressing. There is something about their proportions and their white-painted panelling which makes them intimate and full of charm. One gets a vivid impression in walking through them of courteous, old-fashioned people who were prepared to suffer for their ideals, who never had much money but who had an eye for making their rooms attractive and a little unusual.

The whole house is rich not just with history but with mementoes of its history. The past is lying in layers on the walls. Repairs to the ceiling in the high drawing-room revealed that the original sixteenth-century painted decoration was still there under the eighteenth-century plasterwork; a portion of it has been left exposed. More remains of sixteenth-century painting were uncovered in about

Looking from the house along the long avenue. It leads to the Bear Gates which, according to legend, were closed behind Bonny Prince Charlie in 1745 and will only be opened when a Stuart again reigns on the throne.

Among the relics preserved in the house are the rosary and crucifix of Mary Queen of Scots. The lairds of Traquair were Jacobites and Catholics all through the eighteenth century and suffered for their loyalty to a forbidden dynasty and religion.

Easter Sunday and Monday and from mid-May–September: daily (except Friday) 1.30–5.30. August: daily (except Friday) 10–6. Refreshments by arrangement.

1900 under the wallpaper in the museum room above the high drawing-room. Here dogs are chasing deer and wild boar through lushly intertwining foliage. They help to remind one that in the sixteenth century the hills and forests that still encircle Traquair were alive with game, including bears and wolves and wild boar which have long since become extinct in Scotland.

The museum is full of relics and mementoes, many of them selected from Traquair's rich and still only partly explored collection of family papers. Visitors can see Mary Queen of Scots' prayer-book and rosary and discover how much it cost to be buried in 1759, or what medicines were given to Georgian ladies ('dragon's blood' figures prominently). When they leave the house they can see craftsmen at work in the outbuildings, eat home-made cakes for tea, buy some bottles of delicious home-brewed Traquair ale and depart well satisfied.

Chatsworth

Derbyshire

left Chatsworth from the north-west. A serene and sumptuous façade, water flowing under a graceful bridge, a rich backcloth of woods – for many people Chatsworth is the epitome of a great English country house.

below Table, clock and inkstand of Russian malachite in the music room. The sixth Duke of Devonshire led a mission to Czar Nicholas of Russia in 1826 and the czar presented him with numerous objects of malachite, including a large set of gold cutlery with malachite handles.

It has been said often enough that Chatsworth is a palace – the Palace of the Peak. More lies behind this remark than the fact that it is an enormous building in an enormous park. Chatsworth was built by one of the small group of families who effectively ruled England during much of the seventeenth and eighteenth centuries. As a group they were considerably more powerful than the king; when the king tried to break them, they replaced him with a new one. They had been called the Whig Oligarchy, but they did not think of themselves as an oligarchy in the sense of a small group with absolute power. They genuinely believed that England should be ruled by parliament. But the role of parliament as they saw it was to represent property owners, large and small, not the entire country; and as they owned the most property, it was only right that they should have the most power. But they also believed that power brought responsibilities; they spent much of their life in public service and took care of their tenants and dependants.

Their power was based on the ownership of many thousands of acres, usually spread over several counties, with a separate country house attached to each property and the biggest and grandest house at the centre. The Devonshire Arms inns scattered all over Derbyshire (and many other counties as well) show the extent of the Cavendish empire. It was based on the property left to the Cavendishes by their ancestress Bess of Hardwick in the early seventeenth century, and was always being enlarged as a result of purchase and good marriages. Such property brought the virtual right to a peerage and a seat in the House of Lords, and usually the effective control of a group of MPs, voted for by constituents who were tenants on the family estates. Connections, relatives and friends all brought their own following, and helped to make the Cavendishes, Russells, Grenvilles, Spencers and other great families a power in the land.

The dining-room is one of a suite of enormous new rooms built out to the north of the house to the designs of Jeffry Wyatville for the sixth Duke of Devonshire in the early nineteenth century. While the duke's guests dined they were entertained by his private orchestra, playing in an ante-room next door, and after dinner they could see a play performed in his private theatre.

Chatsworth was transformed from the Elizabethan house built by Bess of Hardwick into the stately building that one sees there today (minus the great wing to the north) at exactly the period when the Cavendishes moved from the second into the first league of power. It all took place during the lifetime of one person. In 1686, at the beginning of the transformation, William Cavendish was fourth Earl of Devonshire and a great landowner, but he was in disgrace with James II, whose Catholic religion and desire for absolute power he disliked and distrusted. A quarrel at court, when he grabbed one of James's courtiers by the nose and laid into him with a stick, had resulted in his being fined £40,000 (which he never paid) and retiring into Derbyshire in disgrace. By the time Chatsworth was finished in 1707 William Cavendish was a duke; he and his friends had turned James II out of the country and brought William of Orange over in his place; he was Lord Lieutenant in Derbyshire and Lord High Steward in London; for the next two hundred years successive Dukes of Devonshire were to have an almost automatic right to a voice in the government and a seat in the cabinet.

The new Chatsworth was a sign of all this, but it was also conditioned by the character of the first duke. He was a man of great charm, very attractive to women; he had a violent temper and a strong sense of the respect due to a duke; he enjoyed horse-racing at least as much as house-building; and he was incapable of planning in advance. When he started to remodel the south front in 1686, he had no intention of doing anything more; but he worked his way round, bit by bit, always on the spur of the moment, frequently disliking something when it was built and having it taken down again. He had an upsetting habit of putting the

Springs on the moors above the house supplied Chatsworth with ample water for ponds, cascades, lakes and fountains, originally installed in the seventeenth century and amplified in the nineteenth. Here the south front is seen across the canal pond, with the Emperor Fountain playing at the far end.

money owing to his builders on a horse at Newmarket and blueing the lot. Although he was immensely rich he was always short of ready cash. Somehow the outside of Chatsworth ended up more or less all of a piece; but the inside was so chaotic that succeeding generations spent many thousands of pounds trying to make it coherent – and perhaps never entirely succeeded.

By the time of the first duke, the towers and huge windows that his ancestress Bess had built at Hardwick had gone completely out of fashion. Pediments, pillars and rich carving derived from the palaces of Italy and France had replaced them as the sign of greatness. Symmetry was still the rule of the day and had been carried to its furthest limits. It was now expected that inside a great house all the doors would be aligned, and outside the grandeur of the house itself was extended by avenues and sheets of water stretching into the far distance.

The south front of Chatsworth, looking along the canal pond and the fountains, was designed in 1686 by William Talman, as was the east front in 1688. The west front, the best-known of all, followed in 1700, but by then the duke had sacked Talman for overcharging him; he may have designed the front himself, or called in Thomas Archer, who certainly designed the north front in 1705. Its curved centre (by which visitors now enter Chatsworth) is a cunning way of concealing the fact that the wall to one side of the curve is several feet in front of the wall to the other. All four façades are built of golden yellow stone enriched by splendid carving; there are Cavendish stags' heads, fitted with real antlers, projecting over all the first-floor windows. The effect is as rich and delicious as treacle pudding.

Inside, the painted hall, two great staircases and the chapel and state rooms on the second floor are the main survivals of the first duke's time. Painted ceilings, carved marble, splendid wrought ironwork and exquisitely carved woodwork make them a good deal more sumptuous than the contemporary rooms in the royal palace of Hampton Court. Much of the decoration was the work of artists and craftsmen brought from London, but much, too, was by local men, especially Samuel Watson from Heanor near Derby. He first appeared at Chatsworth in 1689, working as a young assistant to London carvers; but he stayed on after they had left and for twenty-five years produced exquisite carving in stone, wood or marble, all over Chatsworth including the state apartment. This consists of a series of rooms designed to accommodate a visiting king or dignitary, and a dining-room for great occasions. One can look out of its east window across the lawns and up to one of the first duke's last and most brilliant creations, the cascade. Water brought from the moors tumbles through a little domed temple, spouts up in fountains in front of it, runs right down the hillside by way of a great flight of stone steps and finally vanishes underground near the house.

The first duke died in 1707 and in the next hundred years much changed at Chatsworth. In his time the moors came over the top of the hill behind the house, and the hills across the valley were bleak and treeless. His contemporaries, who were not as addicted to moorland scenery as people are today, described its surroundings as a 'howling wilderness', and they were amazed to find the splendours of Chatsworth marooned in the midst of them. But in the mid-eighteenth century Capability Brown, the great landscape designer, turned the Chatsworth valley into the bower of lush woods and parkland that still sets off the house. The great bridge and stables were built; the entrance was moved from the west front to the north and a new kitchen wing was added; the house was filled with a famous collection of books and paintings, many of them collected by the second duke; and a series of good marriages made the family richer than they had ever been.

By the end of the century social life was changing. Big country houses were no longer mainly planned for the entertainment of a few great people, in richly decorated if not enormously large rooms. Better roads and transport were making it much easier to get around, high society was growing larger as a result of the growing wealth and population of the country, and houses had to cater for huge balls or house-parties in which twenty or thirty people must be kept amused for a week or more.

In 1811 Chatsworth was inherited by William Spencer Cavendish, sixth Duke of Devonshire. He was (and remained) a gay and sociable bachelor. He was kept out of politics by being rather deaf, and unable to hear the speeches in the House of Lords. As he was almost unbelievably rich, it was only natural that much of his energies expressed themselves in altering, enlarging and rebuilding his six country houses, and his houses in London and Brighton. He found Chatsworth extremely inconvenient; the state apartment up on the top floor was too stiff and old-fashioned, too inaccessible for the kind of entertaining he planned and not nearly large enough.

The 'Bachelor Duke' spent forty years and nearly a million pounds (say ten million in today's values) on Chatsworth, and left it much as it is today. He rebuilt the north wing on an enormous scale, using as his architect Jeffry Wyatville, who was later to remodel Windsor Castle for George IV. The rebuilding provided him with a superb sequence of reception rooms running round two sides of the old house and out along the new wing – a music room, two drawing-rooms, a long library, an enormous dining-room, a sculpture gallery fitted with statuary by the best modern sculptors, and an orangery. Up in the tower at the end of the wing was a little theatre, complete with beautifully painted stage sets.

A distinctive feature among the many precious objects which fill the great

above The water supply is channelled along a sham-Roman aqueduct above the house, and from there falls down to feed the cascade. The aqueduct is one of the numerous innovations made by Joseph Paxton, the designer of the Crystal Palace, who was head gardener at Chatsworth for many years.

rooms at Chatsworth, are those made of blue-john or malachite. Blue-john was a local product mined in the Derbyshire hills, but all the emerald-green malachite, sumptuous to the point of vulgarity, is a memento of the duke's friendship with Czar Nicholas of Russia. The duke led an official mission to St Petersburg in 1826 and conducted it with the greatest splendour, largely at his own expense; in return the czar showered him with presents. In 1844 the czar visited England, and in anticipation of a visit the Bachelor Duke prepared the highest fountain in the world at Chatsworth. Several streams up on the moors were diverted, and fed into a big new lake at the top of the hill behind the house, to provide a head of water. The Emperor Fountain as it is called can throw a jet of water two hundred and ninety feet up in the air, and it first played in July 1843. But in fact the czar never came to Chatsworth to see it; he got no further than the duke's house near London at Chiswick.

The fountain was designed and built by the duke's brilliant gardener Joseph Paxton. Paxton came to Chatsworth as head gardener in 1826, aged twenty-two. He arrived there at half-past four on a May morning, when everything was locked up and silent. He toured the whole place, climbing over walls where necessary; set the gardeners to work when they arrived at six o'clock; had the fountains played for him, and went to breakfast with the housekeeper and her young niece, who fell in love with him on the spot and shortly afterwards married him.

Paxton became the duke's adviser, companion and friend as well as his

right The private theatre installed by the sixth duke in his new tower at the end of the north wing. It is the only surviving example of the country-house theatres built as a result of a craze for amateur theatricals in the late eighteenth and early nineteenth centuries.

left The drawing-room is one of a series of magnificent state rooms on the second floor, all of which were decorated when the house was remodelled in the late seventeenth century. The woodcarving is mainly by Samuel Watson, a local craftsman whose work rivalled that of the more famous Grinling Gibbons.

right Two baby carriages under the great stairs. The elegant one on the right dates from the early nineteenth century; the other, gilded and carved with snakes, was designed in about 1730 by William Kent, a brilliant architect who was prepared to design anything from a ball dress to a palace.

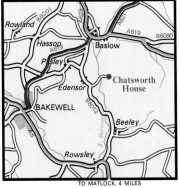

End March–early October: *House* Tuesday–Friday 11.30–4; weekends 1.30–5, Bank Holidays and Good Friday 11.30–5; *Gardens* weekdays 11.30–4.30, weekends 1.30–5.30, Bank Holidays 11.30–5.30; *Farmyard* weekdays 10.30–4.30, weekends 1.30–5.30, Bank Holidays 10.30–5.30.

gardener – and, as the creator of the Crystal Palace in London, a figure of world-wide fame. The gardens at Chatsworth are largely his creation, although elements such as the cascade and canal pond date from the first duke's time. Full-grown trees were transported, great boulders carried down from the moors and expeditions sent all over the world to collect trees and plants. Guests at the duke's house-parties could drive for miles through the park, wander through the apparently endless pleasure grounds, admire the exotic plants in the hot-houses and return to the house for a show in the theatre, or a concert from the duke's private orchestra, followed by a candlelit dinner off gold plate in the great dining-room.

Many of the pleasures of Chatsworth could also be enjoyed by ordinary people, for it has always been open to the public; but the row of baby carriages under the great staircase remind one that it was always a family house as well. There were and are more intimate private rooms (not shown to the public) along the west front. It is still a family house with a living tradition, and almost every year a new feature is added to its attractions or an old one carefully restored.

Castle Howard is a golden and magical place, and also a remarkably unlikely one. For on the face of it it was a crazy idea for a north country earl to try to transform a rather bleak slice of Yorkshire into an outpost of Italy, with a palace in the middle of it rather grander than anything owned by the king of England at the time. It becomes even more crazy when one realizes that he chose as his architect someone who had never designed a building before in his life.

The north country earl was Charles Howard, third Earl of Carlisle. He was descended from 'Belted Will' Howard, a younger son of the Duke of Norfolk, whose marriage to the heiress of Lord Dacre had brought him large northern properties in Yorkshire, Northumberland and Cumberland. The third earl owned castles at Naworth in Cumberland and Henderskelfe in Yorkshire, but in 1693 Henderskelfe Castle was destroyed by fire. He decided to rebuild it, and went for designs to the most fashionable architect of the day William Talman. But Talman was his own worst enemy. In spite of his undoubted talents (of which Chatsworth is the best surviving example), he seems to have been an unattractive character, jealous, quarrelsome, intriguing and big-headed. He produced handsome classical designs for Lord Carlisle, but the two men fell out, and in the end Talman went to law with Lord Carlisle for the money he claimed was owed him for his abortive work. Meanwhile he had been superseded by John Vanbrugh.

Vanbrugh's story is an extraordinary one. He was half-English, half-Flemish by origin: his grandfather was a Flemish merchant Giles Van Brugg who had settled in England; and his father became a sugar merchant in Chester and married a well-connected English wife. John Vanbrugh was born in 1664 and went into the army in 1686. He became a lieutenant in the Earl of Huntingdon's regiment, but resigned his commission a year or two later because his regiment was being sent to Guernsey, and he thought garrison duty on a little island would be tedious. Instead he embarked on a mysterious expedition to France, which resulted in his being arrested as a spy in Calais in 1690 and spending eighteen months in prison there, ending up in the Bastille.

When he was finally released he went back into the army. But in 1697 Captain Vanbrugh surprised London society by writing the play of the year, *The Relapse, or Virtue in Danger*. It was bawdy, lively and extremely funny – just like Vanbrugh

left The south front of Castle Howard, seen across the garden. The house and all the many buildings in the park are built of a local stone that mellows to a rich gold.

right A bird's-eye view of Castle Howard as Vanbrugh planned to complete it. The elaborate gateways leading into the forecourt, and the wing to the right which was to have contained the stables, were never built.

himself. Vanbrugh continued to write plays for the rest of his life. He became a popular figure in smart society, and the boon-companion of the Whig noblemen who were the most powerful group in England. He was a member of the Kit-cat Club, a dining club composed partly of grand Whigs and partly of artists and writers.

The Earl of Carlisle was another Kit-cat member. He struck up a friendship with Vanbrugh which lasted the rest of their lives. In 1699 the captain (then aged thirty-five) must have suggested that the earl let him have a go at designs for his new house.

> Van's genius, without thought or lecture
> Is hugely turned to architecture,

wrote Dean Swift at the time. The captain turned playwright was now turning architect as well – without any training or experience at all. In spite of all the jokes made at the time, the result was triumphantly successful. This was partly because the jovial hard-drinking Vanbrugh was also a genius, and partly because he chose the ideal professional assistant to help him work out his ideas.

This was Nicholas Hawksmoor, who had been assistant to Christopher Wren for fifteen years. Hawksmoor was a diffident and slightly gloomy character who was bad at pushing himself, and was always being passed over for other men. He was not only extremely competent and professional, however, he was an architect of genius in his own right, as was to be shown when he later designed buildings of his own. He was invaluable to Vanbrugh at Castle Howard; just how much he contributed will never be known for certain. But Vanbrugh was so full of ideas and creative energy himself that there is little doubt that Castle Howard is essentially his house – with important contributions from Hawksmoor.

Castle Howard was the new name given to the new house, perhaps to underline the fact that it was built on a new site. The old castle, and Talman's designs for its replacement, had faced east and west, a little to the south of the present house. Vanbrugh built his house on the crest of the hill, facing north and south, with the entrance front looking down the hill to where the great lake now reflects its façade.

Vanbrugh was a dramatist and the north front is essentially dramatic – a series of incidents leading to a culminating moment. Nothing quite like it had been seen in England before, or for that matter in Europe. What Vanbrugh did was to take all the necessary elements of a great country house and, instead of hiding away the less grand ones, make them play their parts in the drama. The bakehouse, the

above One of the most evocative and unusual features of British country houses is the exotic little buildings which are frequently scattered over their parks. Castle Howard has one of the best collections of all. It includes a temple, a bridge, a column, an obelisk, sham fortifications and the pyramid shown above, which was designed by Nicholas Hawksmoor in 1728.

right The chapel, originally fitted out in the 1820s, was richly redecorated in the 1870s. The glowing stained glass was designed by Edward Burne-Jones for Morris and Company, whose decorative wallpapers were being installed by artistic house-owners all over England.

left The north front rising over the lake in the evening midsummer sun. The architect Sir John Vanbrugh changed the site originally chosen for the new house for one which made the best use of his genius for drama and silhouette.

brewhouse, the laundries, the stables and the kitchen were designed to stretch out to either side of the main building in a series of domed and turreted outworks; the house then worked its way inwards through subsidiary wings to the great state rooms at the centre, where a gilded dome, visible all over the countryside, sailed over the whole building.

This countryside was not left as Vanbrugh and Lord Carlisle found it, however. They transformed the original, as Vanbrugh described it 'bushes, bogs and briars', into a mellow and peaceful landscape, with avenues of limes to the west of the house, and to the east wide stretches of open grassland, clumps of trees at the top of the low hills and a string of ponds curving along the bottom of a little valley to the south-east. In the second half of his life the third earl's interests seem, in fact, to have shifted from the house to its surroundings. He never built the chapel and stable wing designed by Vanbrugh as the western third of his great design. Instead he employed Vanbrugh and Hawksmoor to decorate the park with buildings of all kinds. These make up much of the magic of Castle Howard today, and their richness and individuality reflect Vanbrugh's own imagination. Although he was in love with the idea of Italy (which he never actually visited) and with temples

71

left The Temple of the Four Winds was designed by Vanbrugh in 1724–6. It looks north-west to the house and south-east to the mausoleum. Inside, a richly decorated room under the dome was intended for refreshments and summer meals.

and landscapes flooded with the golden light which he knew from Italian paintings, he also loved the bold craggy grandeur of castles and the masculine vitality of the north of England (which he contrasted to what he called 'the tame sneaking south of England'). In spite of its Italian columns, pediments and towers there is more of a castle about the long hilltop silhouette of Castle Howard than its name; and the buildings in the park include castle gatehouses and fortifications as well as Roman temples and columns, a pyramid and a bridge. Among the Roman buildings is one of the most beautiful in England and some would say in the world – the family mausoleum, designed by Hawksmoor, not Vanbrugh, in the form of a huge and gravely magnificent circular temple crowning the top of a hill.

But however much Castle Howard owes to Vanbrugh, Hawksmoor and the third earl, like most English country houses it is the creation of many generations. In the 1750s the fourth earl built the missing west wing, to the designs of his brother-in-law Sir Thomas Robinson. Members of his generation were then in the usual state of reaction against everything done by the generation before them. So Robinson completely ignored Vanbrugh's great design; he followed the Palladian style of the day which was much less dramatic than Vanbrugh's, although, for those who know about classical architecture, very much more 'correct'. (For instance, Vanbrugh had broken all the rules by having Doric pilasters on one side of his house and Corinthian on the other, instead of using the same type all the way round. Hawksmoor commented that it didn't matter – it was impossible to see both sides at the same time.)

The fourth earl's son succeeded as fifth earl and owner of Castle Howard in 1758 at the age of ten and lived until 1825. His early years were crippled by gambling debts contracted when he was a fast young man, moving in the circles of Charles James Fox and the Prince Regent (he is said to have tried to 'introduce the foreign foppery of red heels' into England). But in later years he became a distinguished and enlightened politician and did much for Castle Howard. In the 1770s he built the stable block, a few hundred yards west of the house, to the designs of Carr of York; it now contains a fine collection of costumes of all dates, which is rearranged every year. In about 1800 he fitted up the fourth earl's west wing, which had stood an unfinished shell for many years; and he and the fourth earl between them bought most of the furniture, pictures, statuary and china which still fill the rooms at Castle Howard.

right Looking down into the hall, under the great dome. It is like a dramatic slice of a baroque cathedral inserted into an English house.

below A late eighteenth-century bed in a bedroom in the west wing. The pretty materials and hangings, the comfortable chaise-longue and the well-appointed writing-table are typical of the way the best bedrooms of country houses were furnished in Victorian and Edwardian days.

left The gallery, as painted by
John Jackson c.1810, shortly
after it had been equipped to
take the fifth earl's collections.
The earl and his son,
surrounded by splendid
portraits, busts, and pieces of
furniture, are seen admiring a
picture.

The third, fourth and fifth earls (with, of course, Vanbrugh) remain the dominating presences inside the house, but the work of Vanbrugh and the third earl has suffered from the disastrous fire of 1940 (when the house was occupied by a girls' school). The dome was destroyed, the hall blackened, and the great saloon on the first floor and more than half of the state rooms along the south front were gutted.

Vanbrugh's hall, which survives, with the dome splendidly restored above it, is one of the most exciting country-house interiors in England. Instead of being enclosed by walls and a ceiling in the conventional manner, it breaks out in all directions – upwards into the dome, and sideways through arches to the staircases that led up to the saloon on the first floor, and into the long, vaulted corridors that run behind the state rooms. Wrought ironwork, marbling, gilding and carving add to what has been described as its 'sumptuous gaiety'; Vanbrugh must have thoroughly enjoyed himself working it all out.

From the hall the remaining Vanbrugh state rooms lead up to the fifth earl's great gallery in the west wing. These rooms, and the hall in the west wing by which tourists enter the house, are filled with precious things: family portraits by Reynolds, Lawrence, Lely and others, Dutch and Italian pictures collected by the fifth earl, and classical marbles and mosaics sent back by the fourth earl from Rome, where he lived for many years.

Two other features of the interior of the house need to be mentioned: the bedrooms along one side of the west wing, which are the first rooms shown today to visitors, and the chapel, which is the last. The bedrooms (which were mostly decorated in the early nineteenth century) are delightfully comfortable and pretty rooms, spacious but not too large, and their contents are attractive but not grand; they make it easy to understand why the comfort and elegance of English country houses were the envy of all visiting foreign nobility in the nineteenth century. The chapel dates from the early nineteenth century but was completely re-done in the 1870s. It is an example of Victorian taste at its most discriminating – glowing with decoration and colour in the manner of, and some of it actually by, William Morris and Edward Burne-Jones. Both of them were friends of George Howard, who succeeded his uncle as sixth earl in 1889 and was the friend of many artists and writers, and a talented artist himself.

When he died in 1911 the Carlisle estates were split into two. The earldom and Naworth Castle went to the eldest son, and Castle Howard to a younger son Geoffrey. It is his son George Howard who lives at Castle Howard today, and has done so much to revive its glories since the fire of 1940.

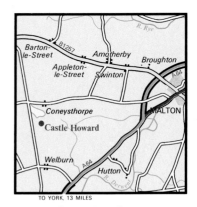

25 March–31 October: *Grounds* daily 10.30–5; *House and Costume Galleries* daily 11.30–5, Bank Holiday Monday 11–5. Restaurant.

Blair Castle
Perthshire

Blair Castle
Perthshire

Since John Cumming of Badenoch first built a tower there in 1269 Blair Castle has had an eventful history. It has been besieged, four times occupied by its enemies, added to, partly destroyed, turned from a castle into a house and back into a castle again. When Mary Queen of Scots went there three hundred and sixty red deer and five wolves were killed at a hunt held in her honour. In 1644 the gallant Cavalier Marquess of Montrose hoisted his standard there. Victoria and Albert were there in 1844, and showered their hosts with presents.

Above all, though, Blair is a vivid reminder of how all great Highland leaders were pulled in two directions. The Earls, Marquesses and Dukes of Atholl were hereditary leaders of the Athollmen. They were feudal chieftains with thousands of loyal, Gaelic-speaking clansmen ready to follow them into battle. Because of their power and position they inevitably got involved in politics. What kind of relationship should Scotland have with England, and the Highlands with the Lowlands? Should they keep to the old ways and loyalties, or move on to new ones? After 1688, when James II lost his throne to William of Orange, and even more after 1714, when the German Georges came from Hanover to reign in London, the situation was polarized. There was the reigning government and king in London on the one hand, and the exiled Stuarts in France, hoping and planning to win their throne back again, on the other.

The safest course was to go in with the government; but the families who did so were not always moved entirely by self-interest. The south could offer all that was new and progressive – the latest ideas and fashions in everything from farming to furniture. A chieftain who tried to strengthen the links between Scotland and England, and bring southern ways up to the north, could feel that he was allying himself with the forces of progress and civilization, and pulling his people out of a barbaric backwater into the main stream. And yet – in doing so was he betraying the traditions of his family and clan, and the loyalty due to the Scottish Stuarts?

The dilemma was a painful one. Some families went one way, some the other. The Murrays of Blair Castle and Atholl went both ways. In the 1715 revolt the first Duke of Atholl and his second son Lord James Murray followed George I. His eldest son the Marquess of Tullibardine and two more sons Lords Charles and George Murray followed the Old Pretender. The revolt failed. Lord Tullibardine went into exile, and on his father's death the dukedom was given to his younger brother. The situation was repeated even more dramatically in 1745 when Prince Charles Edward, the Young Pretender, landed in Scotland and rallied the Highlanders to the Stuart cause. Lord Tullibardine landed with him, and became general of a Highland army. His brother, the second duke, declared for the Georges. Prince Charles and Lord Tullibardine marched south, occupying Blair Castle for a few days on the way. Then Hanoverian troops moved in and garrisoned the castle for the government. Meanwhile Lord George Murray had once again joined the Stuarts; he raised what was called the 'Atholl Brigade' and laid siege to his brother's castle (although his brother was not actually inside it). Blair Castle was in fact the last castle in the British Isles to be besieged. This revolt also failed. Both Lord Tullibardine and Lord George Murray died in exile.

All lost causes are romantic, and loyalty to a lost cause is a quality that appeals to almost everyone. Perhaps the most evocative room in Blair Castle is the little bedroom on the second floor, now consecrated to the memory of the two Jacobite brothers, with its tartan-covered tent bed, its worn tartan carpet and Jacobite portraits on walls covered with faded leather hangings. But it was the Whig

preceding page The castle from the east. It started as a Scottish castle, became a Georgian country house in the eighteenth century, and was re-castellated in the nineteenth. The standard of its owner, the Duke of Atholl, flies from the tower.

76

The tapestry room, one of the suite of richly furnished rooms on the top floor of the castle. The late seventeenth-century bed is hung with red Spitalfields silk and surmounted by four plumes of ostrich feathers. It was originally made for the first Duke of Atholl's apartment in the royal palace of Holyrood, in Edinburgh. Such splendid beds date from the days when a bedroom was used for receiving guests and for christenings as well as for sleeping in.

brother, the second Duke of Atholl, who left his special mark on the castle.

Blair Castle when he inherited it consisted of an old tower known as Cumming's tower, to which a wing and a second tower had been added in the seventeenth century, still in the traditional Scottish castle style. The second duke set to work with enthusiasm to bring it all up to date. He had started before the excitements of the '45, but most of what he did dated from the twelve years that followed it. He removed the old turrets, put in new sash windows, and turned the old castle into a modern country house surrounded by an English-style park. All the rooms were redecorated. Marble chimney-pieces and crate after crate of new furniture were sent up by boat from London to Perth, and then carted by horse overland to Blair. A plasterer called Clayton covered walls and ceilings with lavish stucco decoration in the latest rococo fashion. An entire staircase was made in London by a carpenter called Abraham Swan, and transported in sections up to Scotland.

As a result of the second duke's alterations this Scottish Highland castle became – and remains – a treasure-house of mid-eighteenth-century English furniture and decoration. The best of this is in the main rooms on the first and second floors. The grandest room is in fact on the second floor and had originally been a state dining-room, but the eighteenth-century redecoration converted it into a drawing-room. It is approached by Abraham Swan's grand staircase which rises through

three storeys. At the other end of the house a smaller staircase, known as the picture staircase, leads to the second floor only.

The drawing-room is a stately and spacious room hung with crimson damask; the fact that it is immediately under the castle roof allows it to have a lofty, coved ceiling, rich with splendid plasterwork. The green and white dining-room below is lower and not quite so large, but still very splendid. Its plasterwork is the most sumptuous in the house – culminating in a riotous arrangement of arms and armour over the chimney-piece. The second duke's furniture in this and the adjoining rooms includes Chippendale-style mahogany chairs and tables, ponderous sideboards in the style of William Kent, a four-poster bed hung with red silk, many gilded rococo mirrors and wall brackets, and a gilded bust of the second duke himself, surveying the portraits of his Whig friends in the red bedroom. But the finest bed in the castle belonged to the first duke. It is a state bed of the time of William and Mary, hung with red Spitalfields silk richly tricked out with braid and tassels of faded gold thread, and its canopy is crowned by four great tufts of ostrich feathers. It was made for the first duke's apartment in Holyrood Palace, but was later brought to the tapestry room at Blair – so called because it is hung with Brussels tapestries specially woven for Charles I.

The second duke's time marked the culmination of the Anglophile period at Blair. Later dukes began to go back to Scottish themes and traditions. The wall panels in the second duke's dining-room, which were probably planned to contain family portraits, were filled by the third duke with landscapes of local waterfalls and mountains painted by an Atholl landscape painter Charles Stewart. The same duke went to Perth as well as London for furniture; the attractively mottled furniture which now fills the Derby dressing-room at Blair is made of local broomwood, and was mostly supplied to him by a Perth cabinet-maker called Sandeman.

The third duke had himself and his family painted by a fashionable London painter Johann Zoffany, and, accomplished and delightful though the result was, the portrait could very well have been of an English family in one of the more picturesque parts of England. It is worth comparing with the portrait of the fourth duke and his family painted by the Scottish artist David Allan about thirty years later. Here one is back in the Highlands with a vengeance. The duke is painted as a Highland sportsman, dressed in the full splendour of plumed bonnet, sporran, kilt and tartan stockings. He is standing in front of a dead stag and showing off the blackcock he has just shot to his delighted little daughter. In the background is Blair in its circle of mountains.

The kilt, which was forbidden by law after the '45 Rising, had returned to the Highlands. The main line of the Stuarts had died out; their claim had passed to an obscure Italian prince with no Scottish connections. The Highland chiefs were able to give their undivided loyalty to the reigning English dynasty, but at the same time they became increasingly proud of their Highland traditions. The

above left The third Duke of Atholl and his family, by Johann Zoffany. The racoon in the tree was a family pet, brought from the West Indies by the children's uncle, Lieutenant-Colonel George Anthony Murray.

above The fourth Duke of Atholl and his family, painted by David Allan in about 1810. The duke is wearing the Highland dress which had been forbidden in Scotland in the eighteenth century. Blair Castle in its mountain setting is shown in the background.

right In the dining-room, scenes of the local mountains are framed by lavish baroque plasterwork. Like most of the main rooms in the castle, the dining-room was richly redecorated in the mid-eighteenth century and filled with splendid furniture in the latest style from London.

left The entrance hall dates
from the mid-nineteenth-
century days when Blair was
turned back into a castle. A
portrait of the seventh Duke of
Atholl in Highland dress
surveys a formidable array of
arms and hunting trophies.

culmination of this movement at Blair came in the time of the seventh duke. Blair
became a castle again. In 1869 the Scottish architect David Bryce built up the two
towers, capped them with battlements and 'pepper-pot' turrets, added the tower
through which the castle is now entered, and ran out turreted wings to north and
south. The portrait of the seventh duke presides over his new hall; he is painted as
a Highland chieftain seated before a background of moorland and mountain.

The second duke's Georgian and the seventh duke's Scottish baronial provide,
so to speak, Blair Castle's two main theme songs. But it has much more to offer,
on show in the low vaulted rooms on the ground floor of the castle, in Bryce's
wing and ballroom and in the main rooms on the first and second floors. There are
portraits and pieces of furniture of all periods; there are the rooms furnished for
Victoria and Albert; there are show-cases of old lace and old letters and walls
hung with arms or antlers; and there are books, pieces of armour and ivory,
uniforms, china, clocks, stuffed birds, mantraps, toys, shoes, robes, games and
almost anything else you can think of. There is an ivory spade brought from
Ceylon to England in 1594, and a Victorian necklace and coronet made of deer's
teeth set in enamel. The quality that makes country houses unlike anywhere else
in the world – the gradual accumulation of objects piling up in attics, drawers and
cupboards century after century, pushed out of sight when out of fashion but
never actually thrown away – is nowhere more in evidence than at Blair.

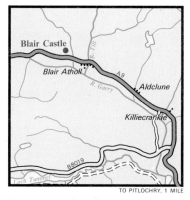

Easter weekend. 1st Sunday in
April–2nd Sunday in October:
weekdays 10–6, Sunday 2–6.
Refreshments available.

Syon House
Greater London

Syon is filled with history. The Britons dug stakes into the river bed here in an attempt to stop Julius Caesar and his legions crossing; one of the actual stakes came to light during dredging and can be seen in the house. There was a famous monastery on the site, founded by Henry V, in order that sixty nuns and twenty priests could pray to God in perpetuity to pardon the king's father for his share in the murder of Richard II. At the Reformation the abbey building passed into secular ownership. Henry VIII's coffin lay there on its way from Westminster to Windsor, and spontaneously burst open during the night. It was there that Lady Jane Grey was foolish enough to accept the offer of the crown from her father-in-law the Duke of Northumberland. Cromwell held a famous council there; and Charles I's children were sent there to avoid the plague.

However there is little feeling of antiquity or history about the house today. The first impression is of an ugly house in a flat park. The park is extraordinary because it has survived as a piece of private open country, with London suburbs hemming it in all round; and there is a gentle charm about its level tree-dotted landscape. But even though the great landscape designer Capability Brown had a go at it, no one could call it one of the great parks of England. As for the house, it is not so much ugly as featureless; and the fact that it was refaced in the nineteenth century means that it does not even look especially old.

The interior transports one into a different world. It is as brilliant as the exterior is pedestrian. In 1758 a young genius called Robert Adam returned to England from four years on the continent. He had met the most advanced architects and artists of the day, and studied the ruins of the great buildings put up by the Romans. He was only twenty-nine, but he set out with complete confidence to revolutionize English architecture, and he succeeded. The Adam style became the rage in London society. Dukes and earls competed to get Adam to build their new houses in London, and to alter or redecorate their great houses in the country. In 1762 Hugh Percy, Earl and soon to be Duke of Northumberland, commissioned him to refashion the interiors of Syon. Adam produced the most brilliant sequence of rooms of his career.

What one sees at Syon today, however, is only half of what Adam originally designed. Syon is built round a courtyard. When Adam came there the range to the south of the courtyard was filled with state rooms and that to the north with family rooms; the north and south ranges were joined by a great hall in the west range and a long gallery in the east range. Adam planned to remodel and redecorate the lot; and in addition to fill most of the courtyard with an enormous circular ballroom. But when he had redecorated the hall, the three rooms of the state apartment and the gallery, the duke decided that he had spent enough money. Adam did nothing to the private rooms in the north range, and the great ballroom was never built. His only other work at Syon was the elegant archway and screen with a Percy lion on top of it, through which passers-by look into the park from London Road.

Much though one may regret what Adam did not do, what he did was splendid enough. His starting points at Syon and elsewhere were the new discoveries being made by archaeologists in the Mediterranean. For centuries 'the grammar of the orders', based on the five traditional orders of Tuscan, Doric, Ionic, Corinthian and Composite, had dominated European architecture. Rules had been laid down and accepted as to what proportions the various orders should have. The system was largely based on the temples, triumphal arches and public buildings which

preceding page Syon House seen across the Thames from Kew Gardens. The lion on its skyline is the crest of the Percy family, Earls and Dukes of Northumberland, who still live at Syon.

right Looking down into the entrance hall over a bronze statue of the Dying Gladiator. The hall is one of the series of reception rooms designed by Robert Adam, whose highly individual style, inspired by the latest archaeological discoveries, revolutionized interior decoration in the 1760s.

survived in and around Rome. But archaeology had now brought to light all sorts of new material. All the time, tombs were being opened and richly decorated urns and sarcophagi dug out of the mud in which they had been hidden for centuries. At Herculaneum and Pompeii whole towns were being stripped of the lava which had buried them; people now knew what Roman shops, club rooms and private houses were like, as well as Roman temples. Roman sites outside Italy were being discovered, recorded and excavated. Adam himself had made an expedition to the great imperial palace of Spalato, in what is now Yugoslavia, and been the first person to make a careful record of its remains, which were so vast that an entire town had grown up inside them.

Roman temples tended to be monumental. The new discoveries revealed a whole new aspect of Rome – luxurious, gay, and full of variety. In contrast to the grave solemnity and massive stonework of the temples, Roman interiors were delicately enriched with small-scale ornament, and painted in a variety of colours. It became clear that the Romans themselves had no qualms about breaking the grammar of the orders when they felt like it, especially in their interiors – even to the extent of inventing new orders.

Adam used these new discoveries as a basis on which to create a brilliant new setting for the English upper classes. He worked on three fronts – colour, contrast and detail. English interiors had been by no means colourless, but there had been little variety in them. Adam decorated his rooms with gay and inventive combinations of all sorts of colours, although he tended to prefer the more delicate pinks, greys, light blues and greens. To prevent them becoming monotonous, he worked out their sequence like a menu; each room was designed to contrast in shape and colour with the ones before and after it, and everywhere he showed an attention to detail and a skill in designing it which has never been surpassed. He designed curtains and carpets, and furniture down to the smallest footstool; he designed ornament of every kind, from sumptuous set-pieces made of arms and armour to sprays and garlands as delicate as a necklace of diamonds.

In Adam's day English high society was at its most brilliant. It was not as stiff as it had been in the seventeenth century, and it was still small enough for everyone to know everyone else. It had an insatiable appetite for enjoyment, and the money to pay for it. In London during the season there were balls and assemblies every night. The inner ring of society, in clothes of matchless elegance and richness, dismounted from their carriages and climbed up splendid staircases to rooms glittering with candlelight and diamonds. In the summer and at Christmas the great families retired to their country houses. But roads were much better than they had been, carriages faster and more comfortable, and country society more sophisticated. The round of entertainment continued.

Adam's architecture vividly suggests this world, and sets it off to perfection. It had its limitations though; it was meant for balls, receptions and formal dinners, and as a setting for graceful minuets, clever repartee and delicately phrased compliments. It was not designed for people who wanted to stroll in from the garden, put up their feet and relax. In fact, upper class tastes were beginning to move in the direction of comfort and informality, rather than courtly elegance, and after fifteen years of being all the vogue, Adam went out of fashion.

His interiors at Syon consist of hall, ante-chamber, dining-room, drawing-room and gallery. They work gradually from magnificence to delicacy, and they oscillate from room to room between cool colours and rich ones. The entrance hall is breathtaking in its combination of architectural grandeur and subtle coolness of colouring. It was designed to set off the noble Roman statues which surround it. Adam's love of what he called 'scenery' and 'movement' is shown in the different ways he treated the two ends. One end is filled with a semi-circular apse, designed to set off a statue of Apollo. At the other a double flight of steps curves behind a bronze statue, the Dying Gladiator, to lead visitors to the state

left The medallions in the red drawing-room ceiling were painted by Cipriani, and show the influence of the Roman painted rooms which were being uncovered in Italy at the time.

right The Elizabethan long gallery was completely redecorated by Adam as a delicate and sparkling room to which the ladies could retire after dinner.

below The ante-room leads off the hall and was designed as a waiting-room for 'superior tradesmen and servants out of livery'. It must have been the most magnificent waiting-room in the world.

rooms. Coming back from the state rooms one looks down into the hall over the silhouette of the gladiator seen from the back, with brilliant effect. Another masterly stroke is the way the bold zigzag of the beams in the ceiling is echoed in the black and white marble floor.

In contrast to the delicate colours of the hall, the ante-room revels in the luxury of gold and marbling. It is designed round some genuine Roman marble columns, which were found in the bed of the Tiber and brought to Syon in 1765. Adam incorporated them into the room, along with copies in scagliola (an imitation marble made of plaster). He surmounted them with gilded statues and filled the gaps between with gilded plaster ornaments on a blue-green background. A gilded ceiling and richly coloured floor complete the decoration and produce one of the most luxurious small rooms in England.

The dining-room is cool again, all cream, pale green and gold. The only dark colouring is in the alcoves, and is used with striking effect to set off the white marble statues which fill them. In contrast the drawing-room is rich with sumptuous fabrics. The original red Spitalfields silk, now much worn, hangs on the walls; the carpet and much of the furniture were designed by Adam, and the ceiling is gaily patterned with octagons enclosing coloured circles.

Adam thought that fabrics were unsuitable in a dining-room because they would 'retain the smell of the victuals', but dining-rooms needed to be splendid because Englishmen of the upper classes spent so much time in them – not only eating, but also talking and drinking after dinner. So 'the eating rooms are considered the apartments of conversation, in which we are to pass a great part of our time'.

In the eighteenth century the gentlemen often spent three or more hours drinking after dinner. Adam envisaged that, meanwhile, the ladies would be sitting in the gallery, insulated by the drawing-room from the noise of the gentlemen as they started on their second or third bottle of port each. So he designed the gallery as essentially a room for the ladies, 'furnished in a style to

above The red drawing-room is still lined with the original silk hangings.

left The dining-room.

House Easter; mid-May – end July weekdays; August – end September daily except Fridays and Saturdays: 1–5. Café, bars and restaurant. *Park* March to October: 10–6; November – February 10–dusk.

offer great variety and amusement'. The room existed before he came on the scene. It was the sixteenth-century gallery and was long, narrow and relatively low (136 feet long, 14 feet wide and 14 feet high). To prevent it seeming too much of a tunnel Adam broke the inside wall up into sections. A section filled with books alternates with a section for a door or a fireplace, between alcoves which originally contained urns and statues (replaced by books at a later date). The whole room sparkled with delicate ornament and scintillated with pale greens and pinks spangled with gold, all now much faded for, unlike the hall and dining-room, the gallery has never been repainted. As 'additional amusement' Adam designed tiny rooms in the turrets at either end – a circular one for china, with a gilded bird-cage hanging from its ceiling, and a square one for miniatures. Unfortunately these are not shown to the public.

After Adam's rooms, the rest of the tour is something of an anti-climax. But visitors should be sure to go on to the gardens. The star piece of the garden centre which has been created in them in recent years is the Great Conservatory, designed by Charles Fowler in about 1830. It is like a Roman temple made transparent. Roofs, domes and much of the walls are filled with a fragile skin of glass and iron, and the result is as gay and delicate in its own way as Adam's dazzling interiors.

3 Personal Reflections

Hardwick Hall
Derbyshire

Most people have heard of Bess of Hardwick, but in spite of her extraordinary life it is unlikely that they would have done so if she hadn't left Hardwick behind to keep her memory green. This was what she intended and she would be pleased, if she returned to life, to see how well her plans had worked out. Hardwick was a blatant but beautiful piece of self-advertisement. Bess's coat of arms or initials stare out in every room – modelled in plaster over the chimney-pieces, embroidered on hangings, bed covers and cushions, or inlaid in the furniture. The six towers that make up its skyline shout out 'ES', 'ES', 'ES' over and over again – the initials of Elizabeth Shrewsbury, silhouetted in stone as part of the parapet. These towers are visible all over the countryside for miles around. The house beneath them, as local schoolchildren are taught, is

> Hardwick Hall
> More glass than wall.

When the low morning or evening sun catches the four storeys of huge windows they light up like a wall of flame, so that it is impossible to ignore them, and they distract the drivers pouring down the M1 motorway in the valley below the house.

At any time, the view of the great house rising from the hilltop above the motorway is an extraordinary one. It is made even more extraordinary because Hardwick consists in fact of two houses. In front of Hardwick New Hall the blackened and craggy ruins of Hardwick Old Hall cling to the steep hillside. The Old Hall is almost as big as the New Hall, and nearly all of it was built by Bess too. But somewhere in the middle of it are the remains of the modest manor house in which Elizabeth Hardwick, the younger daughter of a local squire, was born in about 1525 – four husbands, sixty-five years and an oceanful of experience away from the Elizabeth, Countess of Shrewsbury, who was to build the Hardwick we know today.

Bess's ancestors had been living at Hardwick for several centuries, but in Bess's childhood the family fortunes were in decay, largely because her father had died when she was only a year or two old. England in the mid-sixteenth century was a difficult place for a widow and large family to keep their heads above water – and matters were not improved by Bess's elder brother turning out incompetent and extravagant. Bess was brought up in an atmosphere of worry, near-poverty and fallen family fortunes.

Perhaps the little girl in the decaying manor-house made a vow that whatever happened she would end up rich and famous. At any rate, she accumulated money and possessions throughout her life with dedicated intensity and complete success. She used virtually the only means available to a sixteenth-century woman – marriage, or to be more exact the widowhood that followed marriage. A sixteenth-century wife legally more or less belonged to her husband. He could do what he wanted with the income that came from any property she owned. But once he died she acquired complete control of her own property, and from her husband's a substantial slice of income for life. The proportion was laid down in the marriage settlement; it was usually about a third. Bess had no fortune but she had red hair, a lively wit and tremendous vitality. She married four times. Each husband was grander or richer than the one before. She persuaded two of them to leave her considerably more than the traditional widow's third. She was also

preceding pages The west front of Hardwick Hall. *inset* 'Bess of Hardwick' – Elizabeth Hardwick, Countess of Shrewsbury, in her widowhood.

right The high great chamber. This huge room on the second floor was used for dining in state. The moulded and painted plaster frieze shows the goddess Diana presiding over the animals of the forest.

below Hardwick's windows were filled with glass from Bess's own glassworks and its rooms were decorated with Derbyshire alabaster from her quarries. The alabaster statue of Justice is over a fireplace in the long gallery.

90

clever at tying up her accumulated property in trusts, so that in spite of the law she retained rather more control of it than her existing husband. Moreover she was a brilliant though not always scrupulous businesswoman. She was a money-lender and a farmer on a big scale, had her own leadworks and glassworks, and always employed the best lawyers. When her last and richest husband died in 1590, she scooped the pool and became the wealthiest woman in England after the queen.

Her first husband was Richard Barley, the son of another local squire. They were very young when they married, and he fell ill and died almost immediately. In 1547 she married an elderly civil servant Sir William Cavendish. He had been involved in closing the monasteries under Henry VIII and had made a great deal of money out of it. He and Bess were equally ambitious and came from similar backgrounds. Their marriage, which lasted for ten years, was a successful and very happy one, and the only one of Bess's marriages to result in children. Four years after his death she married Sir William St Loe, a courtier in high favour with Queen Elizabeth. He was a doting husband, but he died only four years after the marriage. Her fourth and much her grandest husband was George Talbot, sixth Earl of Shrewsbury, one of the biggest landowners and most powerful noblemen in England. The marriage brought her a great position, and ultimately a great

fortune, but otherwise was a disaster. After a happy beginning it ended in a quarrel which echoed through England. The Privy Council and even the queen herself endeavoured to put an end to it, with little success. Quite what went wrong has never been established; part of the trouble was that the earl thought Bess had been enriching her Cavendish children at his expense. At any rate, he expelled her from his houses, refused to see her and did his best to keep her short of money.

Towards the end of the earl's life Bess retired to Hardwick. She had bought it from her bankrupt brother in about 1580, and immediately started to rebuild it on as lavish a scale as the earl's harassments would allow. But the moment he died (indeed, when he was still on his deathbed) she started to build a far more magnificent house next door, confident that she now had the means to do so.

Bess's passion for building became famous. She had already built an enormous house at Chatsworth on land bought by Sir William Cavendish. She probably had a hand in an almost equally large house at Worksop, built by the Earl of Shrewsbury. She was later involved in yet another house near Hardwick at Oldcotes, built for her son William Cavendish. All these houses have disappeared, but fortunately Hardwick, in which she had the benefit of a lifetime's experience of building, survives.

At Hardwick she also had a gifted architect to help her. His name was Robert Smythson. To call him an architect is not strictly correct: the profession scarcely existed in Bess's day. He was a master mason who could also draw plans, and had gained a reputation for producing good ones. He had already been involved with Longleat in Wiltshire and Wollaton Hall outside Nottingham. But Hardwick is his masterpiece.

By the time Hardwick was built the taste for symmetry, which could first be seen at Hampton Court, had reached a climax. It was accompanied by another enthusiasm, for enormous windows. Glass was still very expensive, so it became a status symbol and people used it in as large quantities as possible to show how rich

The portrait of Queen Elizabeth in the long gallery was a personal present to Bess from the queen. It hangs on faded tapestry which once belonged to Lord Chancellor Hatton, who won his way to Elizabeth's favour through his skill in dancing.

Like most of the rooms at Hardwick, the blue bedchamber is lined with tapestry. The bed shown here was originally made in 1629 for Christian Bruce, the wife of Bess's grandson William Cavendish, second Earl of Devonshire. In 1601 the room was furnished with a bed embroidered entirely with silver, gold and pearls.

they were. As Bess owned a glassworks she was in a good position to build a house that was 'more glass than wall'. Smythson evolved a plan for her that was as simple as it was effective. Basically Hardwick is a rectangular block round which six towers are arranged at regular intervals, two on each long side and one on each short side. Every side is symmetrical, and the house looks different and exciting from every angle.

Its basic structure would always have made Hardwick an impressive building, but there is much more to it than its structure. Its setting, its decoration and its contents are extraordinary, and Bess's imprint is strong on all of them. She had become a tough and ruthless old woman, but she had a sense of style; and time has mellowed the more ostentatious aspects of her work.

Hardwick is surrounded by walled courtyards and gardens; there are turrets and a gatehouse here and there, and the walls are crowned by long rows of obelisks like great stone spikes, behind which the towers of the house rise mysterious and enclosed. Inside, the rooms are rich in plasterwork and marble – black Derbyshire marble and Derbyshire alabaster brought from Bess's own quarries and carved by her own craftsmen. There are stags everywhere in the decoration, for a stag was the Hardwick crest, and three stags' heads were the Cavendish coat of arms. There are coats of arms everywhere too, those of Bess, of the Cavendishes, and of everyone to whom she or they were connected. Huge heads of helmeted warriors glare at one from over doorways; and in the high great chamber at the top of the house is a wonderful frieze of plasterwork depicting a forest with all sorts of things happening in it – a boar hunt, farmworkers collecting the harvest, a unicorn, the goddess Diana with her court, and deer and elephants paying her homage among the forest trees.

Bess kept what amounted to a little court at Hardwick. The squire's penniless daughter had become a great and powerful person, waited on by gentlemen and gentlewomen, dining in state in her high great chamber, eating off gold plate and being served with elaborate ritual and ceremony. Food for these great dinners

left 166 feet long, 25 feet high, and varying from 22 to 40 feet in width, the long gallery is the largest surviving example of its kind in England. The canopy over the chair comes from a late seventeenth-century bed and was put in its present position by the sixth Duke of Devonshire in about 1830, for picturesque effect rather than use.

right Hardwick is famous for its embroidery, much of it worked by Bess herself and her ladies. A detail from a large hanging shows Mohammed, symbolizing the infidels, prostrate at the feet of Faith. Much of the hanging is made from re-used portions of medieval vestments.

followed a long and dramatic route from the kitchen, and was carried by a procession of gentlemen and yeomen waiters preceded by an usher holding his white wand of office. The procession marched through the hall and up the long, winding stone staircase to the high great chamber, two storeys up from the hall and far away at the other end of the house. By the time it arrived it must have been stone cold, but ceremony mattered more to Elizabethans than convenience.

The grand rooms at Hardwick are all up on the second floor; on the floor below are the rooms where Bess lived, ate and slept when she was not receiving or dining in state; on the ground floor are the kitchens and nurseries. Bess filled the house from top to bottom with splendid things. An inventory made in 1601 shows that almost every room was crowded – with beds and chairs sewn with embroidery and pearls and hung with cloth of gold and silver, with carved and gilded furniture inlaid with marble, with cupboards groaning with gold and silver plate, and with tapestry. Much has disappeared in the course of centuries but a remarkable amount still survives. Tapestry is used almost like wallpaper in the main rooms, and there is wonderful embroidery everywhere. Bess had professional embroiderers to help her, but she loved to do it herself, sitting among her gentlewomen, all busy on their frames. They embroidered coats of arms, stags, animals and flowers of all kinds, and scenes from mythology or daily life, and made them into cushions, table-cloths and hangings for walls or beds.

Bess, like other great Elizabethans, also collected the portraits of her friends, connections and relatives, and of the kings and queens of England. A large number of them are still hanging in her long gallery, next to the high great chamber on the top floor. It is a wonderful room, 166 feet long and 25 feet high, flooded with light from its great windows and lined with tapestry and portraits from end to end. Two portraits of Bess herself hang there – as an attractive young wife in a rich ermine-lined jacket, and as a formidable old widow in black silk and pearls. Queen Elizabeth is there too, wearing an amazing dress glittering with pearls and embroidered with flowers and animals. So is Mary Queen of Scots who was in the custody of Bess and her husband Lord Shrewsbury for fifteen years; she is widely believed to have been imprisoned in Hardwick, although she almost certainly never went there (the New Hall was begun several years after her death). Near her hangs a portrait of Bess's romantic and unfortunate granddaughter Arbella

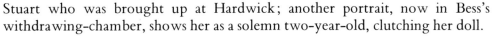

left The long and romantic stone stairs at Hardwick lead from one end of the hall to the second floor. They provided an impressive route for the ceremonial procession carrying each course of a state dinner from the kitchens to the high great chamber.

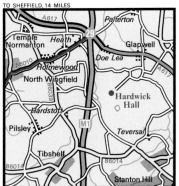

End March–October: *House* Wednesday, Thursday, Saturday, Sunday and Bank Holidays 1–5.30; *Gardens* daily 12–5.30. Refreshments available.

Stuart who was brought up at Hardwick; another portrait, now in Bess's withdrawing-chamber, shows her as a solemn two-year-old, clutching her doll.

There are many later portraits in the long gallery, just as there is later furniture and tapestry scattered all over the house. Bess's descendants, the Cavendishes and Cavendish-Bentincks, became Dukes of Devonshire, Newcastle and Portland, largely on the basis of the wealth and estates which they inherited from her. The Dukes of Devonshire continued to live at Hardwick until it was given to the National Trust in 1956. But they had many other houses, including Chatsworth, so that they seldom spent more than a few weeks a year at Hardwick. This was Hardwick's good fortune; it was carefully maintained but very little altered, so that it has survived into this century as the most complete and romantic of Elizabethan houses.

Blenheim Palace
Oxfordshire

Blenheim Palace
Oxfordshire

Blenheim was built as a gift from the queen and the nation to John Churchill, first Duke of Marlborough. It was a reward for his services, and a commemoration of his victories over the French. Since these had toppled France from her position as the first nation in Europe and put England in her place, there was much to commemorate and be grateful for. Blenheim was at once a monument to national and royal glory, and the home of a national hero.

Everything about it was designed to hammer home the themes of the queen, the duke, victory in war and the defeat of the French. Its name commemorates Marlborough's most famous battle. On the skyline of its two clock towers Grinling Gibbons carved British lions savaging the struggling cock of France. The four pinnacles that rise high into the air from each of the four corner towers of the main building are made up of French *fleurs-de-lys* carved *upside down* under Marlborough's ducal coronet. All the many towers and courtyards of Blenheim are designed to lead up to and culminate in its central mass. This was designed as a final concentrated celebration of victory. Huge trophies of military arms (also carved by Grinling Gibbons) flank the steps that lead up to the main entrance in the great portico. Over its pediment is a statue of Pallas Minerva, the goddess of victory, standing in front of chained French captives. The pediment on the other side of the house was originally meant to support a statue of the duke on horseback, trampling on his struggling French enemies. In the end it was crowned by a rather less dramatic trophy of victory – a bust of the defeated King Louis XIV which was captured by Marlborough in the wars.

Inside, the victorious themes continue. The ceiling of the great stone-lined entrance hall frames an enormous oval painting by Sir James Thornhill. It shows Marlborough dressed as a Roman general displaying a plan of the Battle of

preceding page The west front of Blenheim Palace. The house was built in 1705–20 to the designs of Sir John Vanbrugh, and largely at public expense, as a gift from the nation to the Duke of Marlborough, to celebrate his victories over the French. *inset* John, first Duke of Marlborough, painted by Kneller.

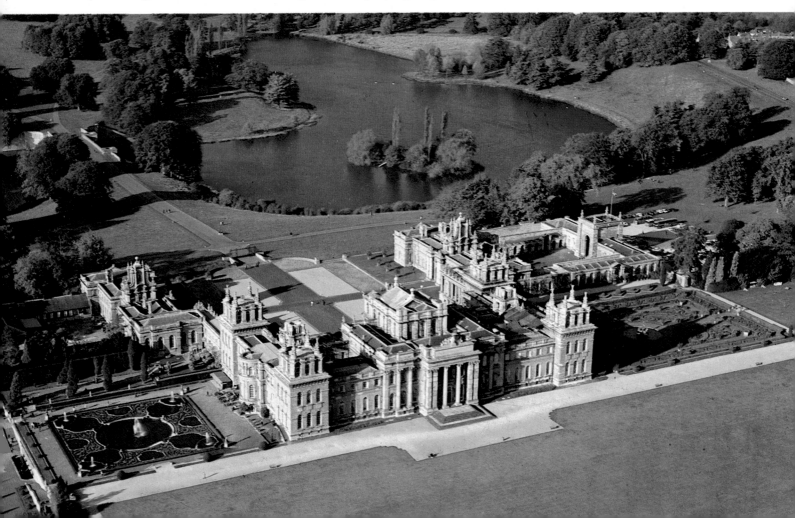

right A great archway at the end of the hall, crowned with the royal arms, frames the bust of the duke under battle standards, a portrait of his benefactress Queen Anne, and the doorway into the saloon.

left Blenheim from the air. The main body of the house lies between the kitchen court, to the right, and the stable court, to the left. The raised portion in the centre lights the great hall, which leads to the saloon on the garden front.

Blenheim to Britannia. Beyond this the great arch at the end of the hall is surmounted by the royal arms, and frames a portrait of Queen Anne above a bust of Marlborough. The door under the bust leads into the lofty saloon. This was designed as a room in which Marlborough could worthily entertain his sovereign. Its painted ceiling shows him riding in triumph in a chariot through the clouds. Over each of the marble doorways is his coat of arms, superimposed on a black double-headed eagle – the crest of the Holy Roman Empire (Britain's ally in the wars) of which he was a prince, as well as being a duke in England. All round the walls the company at dinner was surveyed by a painted crowd of spectators, peering through columns over a painted balustrade. They include a self-portrait of Louis Laguerre, the artist responsible, standing next to the duke's chaplain Dean James, 'whom the duchess disliked but tolerated, because he could make the duke laugh, and would take a hand at cards'.

If the double doors leading from the saloon to the hall and from the hall to the main courtyard are thrown open, one can look in a direct line through hall, courtyard and gates and along the long avenue, which crosses the lake by a bridge as magnificent in scale as everything else at Blenheim, to a column at the top of the hill nearly three-quarters of a mile away. A long inscription at its base recounts Marlborough's victories; and Marlborough himself stands on top of the column, once again dressed as a Roman general, with his hand raised high in a victory salute.

To either side of the saloon were originally self-contained suites of three richly decorated rooms – an ante-chamber, a withdrawing-chamber and a bedchamber.

These were designed as two state apartments in which sovereign and consort could be installed with suitable dignity if they came to stay at Blenheim. The duke and duchess lived in a wing to one side of this, each with their own rather less grand apartment. The matching wing was filled with an enormous gallery (now a library) in which hung the great collection of pictures which Marlborough won by conquest in the wars.

There are tapestries depicting his many victories on the walls of the state apartments. A statue of his monarch and benefactor Queen Anne looks down the hundred-and-eighty-foot length of the library; in the chapel beyond it is Marlborough's tomb and monument. His marble statue stands in Roman armour, crowned with the laurel wreath of victory above statues of History and Fame. Envy, in the form of a hissing dragon, is being crushed under the marble sarcophagus; and the base of the tomb is carved with a relief showing the French marshal, Tallard, surrendering to Marlborough after the Battle of Blenheim.

The purpose of all this needs to be remembered when one visits Blenheim and perhaps finds it an unhomely kind of place. And one has to remember too that although later national heroes would probably have found it embarrassing to be made to live in a monument to their own glories, the first Duke of Marlborough took it in his stride. In his day all dukes and earls took it for granted that they had to live at least part of the time in state. They considered it necessary in order to maintain their power and keep up their position. Even at their own expense they constructed splendid suites of rooms in which to entertain the king or queen, and commissioned statues and frescoes in which they were shown as Roman heroes being applauded by gods and goddesses. They could move through this kind of scene without self-consciousness and change gear quite naturally from the stately deportment considered necessary on great occasions to their moments of relaxation, when they went hunting or played cards and gossiped in their own private apartment.

left Looking over the lake to the north front of Blenheim.

right The walls and ceiling of the saloon were decorated by Louis Laguerre. Painted spectators, including a self-portrait of the artist, gaze through painted columns at the company at dinner.

below The sensational organ at the end of the long library on the west front was installed in 1891 by the eighth duke and his American wife Lilian.

It was a piece of great good fortune that in 1704, when the decision to build Blenheim was taken, the architect who could best respond to this kind of commission had just come on the scene. By then John Vanbrugh had nearly finished the great house at Castle Howard. No one who saw it could have any doubt that he was the man for Blenheim. Once again loyally supported by Hawksmoor, Vanbrugh built up the huge complex like a great orchestral composition transformed into stone. He carried the arrangement he had worked out for Castle Howard even further. He put all the state and family rooms, bedrooms included, on the ground floor, and arranged stables and kitchen in separate wings which formed part of the whole composition. The huge extent of building which resulted was made a unity by Vanbrugh's unfailing gift for silhouette and composition. The ever-changing skyline of Blenheim's nine towers is unforgettable.

As almost always happens with enterprises on the grand scale, nothing quite worked out as intended, however; politics and personalities dragged out the time it took to build Blenheim, and building was accompanied by a series of appalling rows. Marlborough never lived to enjoy his house; by the time even the family wing was built he was old and senile. He is said to have gazed sadly at his portrait by Kneller and said, 'There was a man.' He never dined in the saloon, and when he died in 1722 the great rooms were only half-finished.

At the time Blenheim was started Sarah, the strong-willed Duchess of Marlborough, was Queen Anne's closest friend. They addressed each other by

Sir Joshua Reynolds's portrait of the fourth duke and duchess and their family dominates the east wall of the red drawing-room.

nicknames, as 'Mrs Freeman' and 'Mrs Morley'. Sarah used to boss and bully her unmercifully, but the queen was so attached to her that she took it all meekly. Then in 1710 the queen and duchess quarrelled; and partly as a result of this, the Whigs, who supported Marlborough, went out of power and the Tories came in.

The Tories ended the French wars with a peace treaty which Marlborough and the Whigs considered disgracefully favourable to France. Moreover, as far as Blenheim was concerned, the money dried up. When Queen Anne died and the Whigs came back to power with George I more money became available, but not enough. Blenheim had to be finished at the duke's and duchess's own expense.

In effect this meant that the duchess had to supervise and pay for everything in her husband's old age and then in her widowhood. Her own personal tastes were all for simplicity. It was infuriating for her to have to pour out family money to finish something as vast and elaborate as Blenheim; she only did it out of loyalty to her husband. She was a difficult woman at the best of times, and she began to quarrel with Vanbrugh, whom she thought absurdly extravagant. He resigned in a rage in 1716 and wrote the duchess a letter which she never forgave. The work was finished off partly by Hawksmoor and partly (to Vanbrugh's indignation) by James Moore. Moore had made the looking-glasses for Blenheim; he was an excellent glass-maker but no architect. In 1725, when Vanbrugh and his wife tried to visit his greatest masterpiece, now at last complete, the duchess refused even to let them inside the park.

Although the memory of the first duke dominates Blenheim, of course many subsequent dukes have lived there since his day, and most of them have left their mark. Like other country houses Blenheim has changed over the centuries,

J. S. Sargent's portrait of the ninth duke, his American wife, the heiress Consuelo Vanderbilt, and their family was painted to complement Reynolds's group on the opposite wall.

sometimes for the better and sometimes for the worse. The biggest and most successful of the changes came in 1764, in the time of the fourth duke. Up till then Vanbrugh's great bridge had crossed a relatively small stream at the marshy bottom of the valley, but in 1764 the landscape gardener Capability Brown dammed it and made the noble lake that is there today. He is said to have remarked, with some justification, 'the Thames will never forgive me for this'.

The lake, and the trees that set it off, are such a splendid conception that one has to forgive Capability Brown for the less happy changes he made closer to the house. By the middle of the eighteenth century formal gardens had gone completely out of fashion. Brown swept away the elaborate parterre, terraces and avenues which had been laid out in the first duke's time before the south front of Blenheim. In doing so he destroyed the setting designed for the house. The enormous and featureless lawn which replaced it was no compensation.

Changing fashions and life-styles were causing changes inside the house as well, which also destroyed much of the point of Vanbrugh's design. In the late eighteenth and the nineteenth centuries the sets of grand three-roomed suites for royalty or other important visitors, which Vanbrugh had provided to either side of the saloon, were no longer considered necessary. Great people were becoming more like other mortals and no longer expected to be put up in state. What was needed was a series of capacious rooms in which to give balls or entertain large house-parties. Accordingly the great four-poster beds were moved out of the two downstairs state bedrooms at Blenheim and all the rooms run together in a series of reception rooms. The result was not really very successful. The gallery was too large to make a comfortable library, and the rooms to either side of the saloon too

small for drawing-rooms; and Blenheim, grand though it was, was left without enough bedrooms.

above The simple bedroom in which Winston Churchill was born.

The state rooms gradually filled up as the portraits, pictures and furniture acquired by subsequent generations were brought in to supplement the original contents. Perhaps the most memorable of the later additions are the portraits of the fourth and ninth dukes and their families, which look at each other across the red drawing-room. The earlier group is by Reynolds, the later by Sargent. He deliberately set out to rival Reynolds, and succeeded.

The beautiful duchess who dominates this and other portraits at Blenheim was Consuelo Vanderbilt, daughter of one of the most opulent of American millionaires. The ninth duke married her out of a sense of duty to his family; the Marlborough fortunes were in decline and Blenheim was in need of the Vanderbilt millions. Consuelo was pushed into marriage at the age of eighteen by her mother, who liked the idea of a duke as a son-in-law. As both husband and wife were in love with someone else, the marriage was far from successful and broke up after eleven years. Consuelo's memoirs give a fascinating picture of life at Blenheim in late Victorian and Edwardian days. Not surprisingly the duke comes very badly out of them; but in fact he was a remarkable man, and he did a great deal for Blenheim. To east and west of the house he installed formal gardens, which did much to make up for what Capability Brown had taken away. The water-gardens, which run down to the lake from the west front, are amongst the most brilliant and enjoyable examples of garden design in England.

When Consuelo married the duke, his young first cousin Winston was heir to the dukedom. She was told that her first duty was to have a son (she had two) as it would be intolerable if 'that little upstart Winston' were to inherit the title. Times have changed. Winston Churchill is now one of the glories of Blenheim; the unassuming bedroom off the hall in which he was born has become a place of pilgrimage, and the rooms next door to it are now a museum to celebrate the memory of the great duke's most famous descendant.

End March–October: daily 11.30–5. Restaurant.

Stratfield Saye

Hampshire

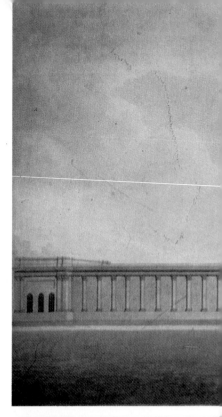

Stratfield Saye
Hampshire

Stratfield Saye makes an interesting comparison with Blenheim. They were both acquired with public money to be the home of a national hero. The Duke of Marlborough and the Duke of Wellington were both military geniuses, who had led the country to victory against the French after long and hard fought wars. Both were, as a result, figures of world renown.

Stratfield Saye is far more modest than Blenheim, yet the interesting thing is that a house on the scale of Blenheim was very nearly built there. The property was bought for the duke in 1817, after he had looked at a number of houses and rejected them. He was much taken by Uppark, but decided against it because the price was too high and the hill too steep. Perhaps one reason why he decided on Stratfield Saye was that it has virtually no hills at all; he was an extremely practical man, and well aware of the speed at which hills would wear out his carriage horses. At first it never occurred to him that he would live permanently in the existing house. Hanging in the corridors of Stratfield Saye is a series of designs for a Waterloo Palace every bit as grand as Blenheim, which was to have been built on a slight eminence to the north-east of the present house. The duke even began to buy marble columns in Rome to incorporate in its decoration.

In the end, however, nothing was built. There just wasn't enough money available for a palace, even though the nation had been generous to the duke and he had been given properties in Belgium, Spain and Portugal as well. Perhaps equally important, the climate of taste and opinion was changing. The duke lived half way between the times when national heroes were expected to live on a heroic scale in monumental houses, and when they were expected to live modestly (and only make a fortune from their memoirs).

So the duke continued to occupy the old house. Although his friends and admirers considered it unworthy of him, he grew very fond of it. He lived on a modest scale for a duke, and only made comparatively minor additions to the house. Stratfield Saye acquired no painted ceilings, with the duke seated among gods and goddesses, or marble statues depicting him as a Roman hero. Such features wouldn't have appeared even if Waterloo Palace had been built; by the nineteenth century this kind of glorification was considered ridiculous in a man's own house, though still just acceptable on his monument.

This is not to say that the face, figure, and exploits of Wellington are not much in evidence at Stratfield Saye. He was still a national hero. He complained bitterly that he had spent the first half of his life earning a world-wide reputation in order to pass the second half sitting for artists and sculptors. He may not have been quite honest about this; certainly he was happy enough to hang the results in his house. Pictures and prints of Wellington and his battles are all over the place, along with every kind of memento of his life and career.

One can see why Wellington developed an affection for Stratfield Saye. It is certainly not a stately house but it has a great deal of character and charm. It was originally a long, low, red-brick house, built in about 1650 by Sir William Pitt, James I's comptroller, and decorated with the so-called 'Flemish gables' (with curved sides and pedimented tops) which were in fashion at the time. Two matching stable blocks front the house and give it a forecourt and a pleasant air of formality.

Nothing of this period survives inside the house, however, except for a couple of staircases. Otherwise it was entirely redecorated by Sir William Pitt's grandson Lord Rivers, so that the seventeenth-century house has Georgian interiors – full of

preceding page Stratfield Saye house and estate were bought by the nation for the great Duke of Wellington in 1817. At first the agreeable but relatively unassuming mid-seventeenth-century house was not considered grand enough for a duke, but plans to rebuild it never materialized. *inset* The first Duke of Wellington, by Benjamin Robert Haydon.

above The decoration in the library dates mainly from about 1740. The splendid lamps, like others in the house, were originally lit by colza-oil, a heavy vegetable oil much used in the 1830s.

top A design by Benjamin Dean Wyatt for rebuilding Stratfield Saye, and making it the Blenheim of the nineteenth century. The columns bought in France and Italy for the proposed palace can be seen today in the conservatory.

charm and also variety, because the rooms were decorated over thirty or forty years in the successive fashions of different decades. Lord Rivers also covered the brick exterior of the house with stucco, the warm orange colouring of which now gives the house much of its charm.

The only important additions Wellington made to the house were a conservatory at one end and a real tennis court in the outbuildings, and he made only minor changes in its decoration. But the contents are almost all his, and many of them reflect his own personal tastes. For instance he loved Dutch pictures, and the fortunes of war had given him a splendid collection of them. After the victory of Vittoria, when he was fighting the French in Spain, he captured the baggage-train of Napoleon's brother Joseph, whom Napoleon had made King of Spain. In it was a great collection of pictures belonging to the Spanish royal family. When King Ferdinand, the legitimate king, was restored to the throne Wellington sent them to him, but they came back by return, with an accompanying letter: 'His Majesty, touched by your delicacy, does not wish to deprive you of that which has come into your possession by means as just as they are honourable.' So Wellington kept the pictures; the best are still in Apsley House, which was his London home, but there are many more at Stratfield Saye.

Apart from the pictures the winnings of his career include much that is sumptuous or exotic, from Napoleon's own uniform to services of plate and china given to him by kings, emperors or admirers. The dining-room table, for instance, is set with a silver and gold service supported on silver elephants, which was presented to him by his officers when he left India in 1805 – having laid the foundations of his fame by his victories against the Indian princes who were supporting Napoleon. In the billiard room is a selection from the famous dinner service originally made at Sèvres for Napoleon to celebrate his conquest of Egypt. It is covered with Egyptian scenes and figures, and has a centre-piece in the form of an Egyptian temple and obelisks.

A fascinating aspect of Stratfield Saye is that, in addition to this exotic booty, almost all Wellington's personal belongings have been carefully preserved as relics of the great man, and visitors today can still see them lying around as though the duke had just walked out of the house. His spectacles, his handkerchiefs, his razor and razor strop, his underclothes (marked with 'W' and a coronet), his carpet slippers and dressing-gown, the little bottle of rosewater with which he used to wash his eyes, the candle-holder and stand over which he used to heat up water when

on campaign, are all on view. A bulging umbrella with a spike on the end reminds one that he had a political career as well as a military one (he was twice prime minister), and that he was not always a popular hero. For the duke did not believe in democracy; he carried the umbrella round with him at the time he was fighting tooth and nail against efforts to reform parliament to make it more representative, and the windows of Apsley House were smashed and his own life endangered as a consequence.

It is a little surprising to find a tough old campaigner like the duke obsessed with precautions against catching cold. He owned an amazing number of nightcaps, flannel mufflers and long-johns; and he did everything he could to keep Stratfield Saye warm. He installed central heating when it was still something of a novelty (two ponderous radiators survive at the bottom of the staircases) and even put in double glazing; he boasted that he kept the temperature to sixty-four degrees even in the halls and staircases.

above left The hall is hung with Napoleonic flags given to the duke when he entered Paris after Waterloo. Mosaic pavements excavated from the nearby Romano-British town of Silchester (*Calleva Atrebatum*) are set into the floor.

above centre The grave of Copenhagen, the horse who carried the duke at Waterloo.

above right The gallery runs behind the hall along the garden front. It glows with dull gold from wallpaper, French furniture, and a splendid series of gilded busts of kings, emperors and generals. The carpet, like others in the house, was woven at the Spanish Royal Carpet Factory in Madrid in the 1950s.

One explanation for this may be that colds increased his deafness and pains in the head. He had suffered from these ever since a so-called specialist poured caustic down his ears in 1822 in an attempt to cure the much-less-total deafness caused by standing too near an exploding gun. His deaf aids are also on view, and his false teeth.

Some of his clothes suggest, perhaps rather unexpectedly, that the duke was a bit of a dandy. A short canvas coat with a brown velvet collar is extraordinarily elegant; so is the cloth coat lined with reindeer skin which he wore in Russia. The popular image of him as the 'Iron Duke' – curt, pithy and unbending, in fact the prototype of the strong silent man – is not the whole truth. He had a strong sense of duty and honour; he was so independent that he brushed his own clothes even when he was an old man, and said he would have liked to clean his shoes as well. But he had other, perhaps more unexpected traits. For instance, his taste in furniture and decoration was for gilt and gaudiness, rather than for the plain good sense one might have expected. The elaborate French furniture in the house was all bought by him, and he chose the French wallpaper in the drawing-rooms – gold flowers on a white ground, gay enough even after more than a hundred years' fading. He also selected the amazing papier mâché billiard-table inlaid with flowers, which is still at Stratfield Saye, and considered it the most beautiful piece of furniture he had ever seen. Another example of his taste is the rooms decorated with prints pasted on to the wallpaper. The gallery was already done in this way when he bought the house, and he liked it so much that he copied it in several other rooms, and took endless trouble in selecting and arranging the prints.

There was nothing he enjoyed more than a good gossip with a clever, sensible, pretty woman. In private company he could be extremely amusing; he had a dry way of putting things. A good example is his advice to a club that was thinking of making bishops eligible for membership: 'If you let in the bishops, mind your umbrellas.' The notice still on display in the porch of the house was certainly written by him: 'Those desirous of seeing the house are requested to ring at the entrance and to express their desires. It is wished that the present practice of stopping on the paved walk to look in at the windows should be discontinued.'

The first duke was a national hero for many decades before his death in 1852, and almost everything to do with him was carefully preserved. There is a display of his clothes on show in the Wellington museum which has been created in the stables. It includes shirts, underclothes, nightcaps and carpet slippers. Other personal relics of Wellington on show at Stratfield Saye range from his umbrella to his false teeth – and, of course, his Wellington boots.

Unfortunately, the duke's own wife was neither clever, sensible nor pretty. She was gentle, loving and generous, but scared stiff of the duke, and their marriage was not a happy one. There is very little to remind one of her in the house today. Her rooms were on the first floor at the north-east corner of the house, and the duke's rooms on the ground floor at the south-west corner. This just about sums up their relationship.

The duke's rooms are not shown to the public (they are in the part lived in by the present duke and his family). His personal possessions are now mostly on view in a beautifully arranged Wellington museum which has been formed in the stables. There are more Wellington mementoes in the grounds, including many of the conifers now known as wellingtonias (which were named in his honour the year after his death) and the tomb of his charger Copenhagen. The thought of the veteran duke raising a monument to the gallant old horse who had carried him at Waterloo is a touching one, but in fact England's greatest man had none of the English love for animals; he loved children, but not dogs or horses. The monument was put up by the second duke; the great duke could not even remember where Copenhagen had been buried.

The dining-room is hung with portraits of Wellington and his family. They are dominated by Thomas Hoppner's superb portrait of the duke as a young major-general in India, where he made his reputation fighting against the coalition of Indian princes who supported Napoleon. The dining-room table is set with the silver and silver-gilt service presented to him by his officers at the end of his Indian campaign. It includes sweetmeat bowls supported on silver-gilt elephants.

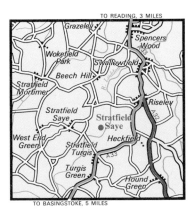

End March–September: *House* daily (except Friday) 11–5.30; *Wellington Country Park*: daily until end November. Refreshments.

Abbotsford
Roxburghshire

Of all the houses described in this section (with the possible exception of Hardwick) Abbotsford is the most personal. Blenheim after all was more a celebration of Marlborough than an expression of his individuality. Waddesdon expressed a family as much as a single person. There is a great deal of Disraeli that does not appear at Hughenden, and of Kipling that does not appear at Bateman's. But Abbotsford expresses all Sir Walter Scott's enthusiasms and tastes, and fulfilled his life-time ambition.

It is also remarkable as being the only instance in the British Isles of a writer – indeed a novelist – making his way into the ranks of the landed gentry, building a great house, buying an estate of over a thousand acres and acquiring a title, all from the winnings of his pen. Other writers may have made as much money but none have chosen to invest it in so socially ambitious a way. Even Alfred, Lord Tennyson never acquired an estate approaching the size of Abbotsford, nor built a house as large.

To call Scott socially ambitious, however, is not strictly accurate, or fair to him. He was socially romantic. All his life he was in love with the Scottish Borders – where his family came from and where much of his youth was spent – and with their traditions, tales and ballads. When he was a young and not especially successful lawyer, with very little money, his happiest and most fruitful days were spent riding in the remoter Border districts, talking to shepherds, farmers and other local people, and writing down from their memory all the old ballads which were beginning to be forgotten. There was no shortage of them, for the wild and lawless days when the Borders were a fighting district, living off pillage from English farms across the hills (or sometimes off pillage from each other), had produced much vivid and stirring poetry. Scott's collections of these ballads were published in 1802, and were the beginning of his reputation. All Border life centred round family clans, faithful to their chief and to the lairds who headed the various branches of the main family. Much of the clan spirit lingered on into the nineteenth century. To Scott nothing could seem more satisfying or romantic than to become a Border laird himself.

To begin with his ambitions did not stretch so far however. After making his collection of ballads Scott went on to write his own poems. They were immediately and outstandingly successful, and made Scott a very comfortable though far from enormous sum of money. For a number of years he rented a house from one of his cousins at Ashiestiel, not far from Abbotsford, but in 1811 his lease was beginning to run out and he decided to buy a small farm of 110 acres on the south bank of the Tweed. It was called Cartleyhole; but because the land had belonged in medieval days to Melrose Abbey, and there was a ford over the Tweed just by the house, he decided to rename it Abbotsford.

The place, even if Scott had been able to buy more land, was not really suitable for a country house and estate on the full scale because it was quite closely hemmed in by a public road on one side and the river on the other. But at this stage Scott's ideas were limited to little more than a country cottage, a retreat from the town house which he already owned in Edinburgh. The farm consisted of a small farmhouse and a barn or steading across the farmyard. Scott and his family lived for a short time in the farmhouse, in great discomfort; then he made a modest addition, four small rooms downstairs and three bedrooms upstairs, between the farmhouse and the steading. A little groups of friends helped him with advice on the design, but it was a far from grand affair.

Looking down to the entrance front of Abbotsford, the house which Sir Walter Scott built with the money earned by his novels. Behind the courtyard in the foreground is the self-contained wing built by Scott's grandson as a refuge from the tourists who flocked from all over the world to visit the house. *inset* Scott and his greyhound Percy. A detail from the portrait by Raeburn.

The house seen from over the River Tweed. Scott called it Abbotsford because the land on which it stands had belonged to the nearby Abbey of Melrose, and a ford just below the house had been used by the monks.

Then his situation changed dramatically. In 1814 Scott decided to try writing novels instead of poetry. His first novel *Waverley* was published anonymously in 1814. It was a best seller, and so were nearly all the novels that followed it – also published anonymously, although the secret of their authorship gradually leaked out. The spread of education and the growth of the middle classes had produced an enormous potential new readership, hungry for romance. Scott recreated for them life in his two favourite districts of Scotland, the Borders and the Highlands, in the eighteenth century (and later made some highly successful excursions into England in medieval and Elizabethan days). His income from sales became by far the biggest literary income of his day.

So Scott was soon in a position to buy more land, enlarge his house, and become a laird in earnest (and ultimately, in 1820, Sir Walter Scott, baronet). He bought another thousand acres, much of it on the other side of the main road, and planted trees all over them with unlimited enthusiasm. Between 1822 and 1824 he pulled down the old farmhouse and replaced it with a grand new wing. The architect was William Atkinson, who had made a reputation by building castles in England. But once again Scott took advice and suggestions from his friends and was always full of ideas himself. The resulting house expressed what he wanted exactly.

The outside of the house is interesting because so many motifs, and a few actual relics, from old Scottish buildings were incorporated into it. The crow-stepped gables and the distinctive little corner turrets, for instance, are both very common in Scottish castles; but no one had thought of incorporating them into new buildings before Scott. He started a fashion which was ultimately to be copied all over Scotland, and to be nicknamed (not always affectionately) Scottish Baronial.

Atkinson was not a very good architect, and Scott was an amateur. From the outside Abbotsford looks rather more like a toy house than a real one; and perhaps the big nineteenth-century windows filled with plate glass don't harmonize all that well with the old-style towers and gables. But inside Abbotsford is completely convincing. Scott was a magpie, and collected and copied all sorts of things as much for their associations as their appearance. Abbotsford inside ought to look a mess because it is made up of so many bits and pieces. The entrance hall, for instance, contains part of Scott's large collection of arms and armour of every sort, date and provenance (there is more in the little

armoury next door); oak panelling and furniture taken out of old houses; relics of
Waterloo; the head of an elk; a stone fireplace copied from the cloisters of
Melrose Abbey; a copy of the skull of Robert the Bruce; and the coats of arms of
the Border clans, of Walter Scott's ancestors and of his friends. And yet it all hangs
together, and makes a room full of individuality and character, partly because all
the bits and pieces reflect different enthusiasms of Scott and partly because they all
merge together into a rich mosaic. The colours are, it is true, limited. Scott, like
others of his generation, liked the sombre richness of brown panelling, and rooms
made dark and a little mysterious (as the hall is) by stained glass. But this is all part
of the character of the house.

Scott's especial territory was the study in which he wrote his books, and the
library next door to it. The study is very much the workshop of a professional
author. It is not large but rather high, and is lined from floor to ceiling with books,
with a gallery half way up to give access to the higher ones. It contains little
furniture except Scott's own comfortable leather chair and his desk, copied from
the desk of a friend (in 1935 two secret drawers were found in the desk, containing
fifty-seven letters between Walter Scott and his wife). The library next door was a
room for his friends as well as for Scott. It has the same rich brown colouring and
book-lined walls but is a very large room, much the largest in the house, with a
great bay window looking down to the Tweed. It must have been a pleasant
room to sit around in.

The drawing-room next door was the only one of the big downstairs rooms
which Lady Scott was allowed to decorate. Its gay Chinese wallpaper makes a
pleasing contrast to the brown-walled rooms around it (the armoury and dining-

room are painted in light colours only because they have been redecorated since
Scott's death). Even here, though, another facet of Scott's personality is in
evidence. The great central candelabrum was originally lit by gas like the rest of
the house, which remained gas-lit until only a few years ago. What appear to be
elaborate little metal urns to either side of the fireplace are in fact air-bells; the
pressing of a plunger sets up pressure in a tube which connects to, and pushes out,
a hammer at the other end, to strike a bell by the servants' hall. In spite of his
enthusiasm for tradition and the past, Scott was also an enthusiast for modern
gadgets. Both air-bells and gas (he used gas made from oil, not coal) were the
latest inventions when he installed them; his son-in-law complained bitterly that
the gas stank, and produced much too garish a light, but Scott loved it. He also put
hot-air heating into the hall (the pierced brass grating, complete with regulator,
through which the hot air rose can still be seen there) and built an icehouse next

left Scott was a dog lover, and Abbotsford is full of mementoes of his numerous dogs. Above is Ginger, painted by Sir Edwin Landseer.

door to the main building, and neatly disguised it with gothic trimmings.

Scott loved Abbotsford, spent much of his time there and entertained constantly. He was a delightful man, unassuming, generous, high-principled and full of fun. He was never happier than when working in his woods alongside his foresters, wielding an axe himself with considerable skill; or walking through the woods with the series of dogs, large and small, whom he loved as friends, and who appear in portraits or effigy all over Abbotsford. But he was equally at home at a dinner table crowded with brilliant guests, or surrounded by his own family.

Then, in 1826, disaster struck him. For many years he had been a partner in the Edinburgh printing firm of John Ballantyne and Co. In more recent times he had become very much a sleeping partner and had not paid as much attention as he should to the way the firm was being run. It had become involved with the London (Scottish by origin) publisher Archibald Constable, who failed in 1826 and brought Ballantyne's down with him. Scott, at the age of fifty-five, found himself faced with liabilities of £116,000 (well over a million in modern money). He could have gone bankrupt, but he refused to do so. He came to an agreement with his creditors, sold his house in Edinburgh, reduced his staff at Abbotsford to what (in those more expansive days) was considered a minimum, and set out to earn the money to pay off his debts.

The cheerfulness with which he accepted the disaster, and the honourable way in which he took the debt on himself, showed Scott at his very best. But the whole business shed considerable gloom over his last years, and possibly hastened his death. He died in 1832, in the dining-room at Abbotsford.

Well before he died, Abbotsford had become a place of pilgrimage. Bunches of tourists were always intruding on Scott's privacy; and countless pictures, engravings, bits of china and other souvenirs and mementoes, made before Scott's death and after, made Abbotsford as familiar as Osborne or Windsor Castle. After he died, the house was regularly open to the public; so much so that James Robert Hope Scott, who married Sir Walter's granddaughter, built a new wing on to one side in which he could live in privacy, away from the tourists. His descendants live there still.

End March–October: weekdays 10–5; Sunday 2–5. Private entrance for disabled visitors. Teashop.

Waddesdon Manor

Buckinghamshire

Waddesdon Manor
Buckinghamshore

People who drive around Buckinghamshire can scarcely help noticing the distinctive symbol which appears on a large number of Buckinghamshire buildings. It consists of five arrows bound in a sheaf together. It is the crest of the Rothschilds. The houses, cottages, stables and farm buildings on which it occurs are almost always more solidly and lavishly built than similar buildings without the crest. As someone once put it, 'to be a Rothschild horse or dog was considered an enviable distinction among more plebeian quadrupeds'. The cows at Lord Rothschild's house at Tring were said to eat out of silver mangers. The story was probably untrue – the Rothschilds tended to attract legends – but it *was* true that Lord Rothschild's brother Alfred used to drive around in a pony-cart pulled by zebras. He belonged to the third generation of the family, when it could afford to be eccentric as well as rich.

The five arrows of the crest stood for the five original Rothschild brothers. They were the sons of a Jewish dealer in coins and medals operating in Frankfurt, who had developed his business into a banking house. By 1800 the five sons had spread over Europe. They each had their own banking house, in Frankfurt, Vienna, London, Naples and Paris. Between them they dominated European finance and their combined wealth was fabulous.

During the nineteenth century the Rothschilds increased and prospered. They became less of a phenomenon and more of an institution. As a family they stuck together. They tended to marry other Rothschilds; it was a useful way of keeping the money in the family. They moved easily from country to country, wherever there were more Rothschilds. They built houses all over Europe, and filled them with precious things.

In England they were clannish in their houses as well as their wives. In London they all lived in opulent mansions either in or near what became known as 'Rothschild Row' – the west end of Piccadilly. In the country they settled around Aylesbury, all within from two to twelve miles of each other. Between them they owned about thirty thousand acres, in Buckinghamshire or just across the border in Hertfordshire. They ran a pack of hounds, numerous model farms

preceding page At the peak of their fame and wealth in the second half of the nineteenth century the Rothschilds built lavishly all over Europe. In England they scattered the Vale of Aylesbury with country houses, of which Waddesdon is the most magnificent. It was designed in *château* style by a French architect G.H. Destailleur and built in 1874–89. *inset* Baron Ferdinand de Rothschild, the builder of Waddesdon.

right The entrance front of Waddesdon from one of the fountain ponds. Half-grown trees were dragged by teams of horses or cable engine to the house's bare hilltop site in order to produce a mature setting in the fastest possible time.

below A simplified version of the immensely complicated Rothschild family tree, showing the Rothschilds in England (underlined in red) and their houses.

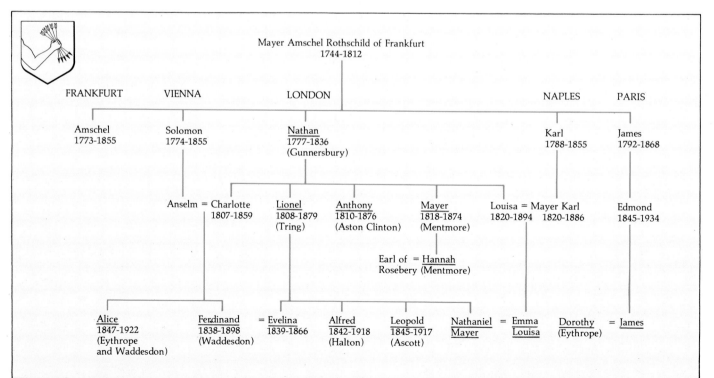

and several racing stables; they represented the area in parliament for nearly sixty years; and any local cause could be certain of generous Rothschild cheques. There were seven Rothschild houses in the area, none of them small and three of them enormous. Baron Meyer and Baron Leopold settled at Mentmore and Ascott to the north of Aylesbury; Baron Alfred, Sir Anthony and Sir Nathan (later Lord Rothschild) at Halton, Aston Clinton and Tring to the east; and Baron Ferdinand and his sister Miss Alice at Waddesdon and Eythrope to the west.

Baron Ferdinand belonged to the Austrian branch of the family, but his mother was an English Rothschild and so was his wife. He left Austria for England as a young man, and stayed there even after his wife died in childbirth after eighteen months of blissfully happy marriage. It was as a childless widower that he set to work to build the biggest and best of the Rothschild houses.

The Duke of Marlborough was short of money as a result of the great agricultural depression of the late 1870s (Vanderbilt millions for Blenheim were still in the future). He sold Baron Ferdinand a bleak hilltop at Waddesdon and several hundred acres round it. At once, to the amazement of the locals, things began to happen. A special railway line was built to carry Bath stone to the bottom of the hill. Teams of cart-horses were imported from Normandy to drag the stone up to the top. Its bleakness disappeared as hundreds of full-grown trees were hauled into position and planted on its slopes. And on the crest of the hill there gradually rose – a French *château*, or, to be accurate, several French *châteaux* rolled into one. A knowledgeable eye can distinguish substantial chunks of Chambord, Blois and other famous French houses incorporated into Waddesdon. The baron had been visiting the *châteaux* of the Loire and had come back full of enthusiasm for their architecture – and with a French architect and a French landscape-designer to turn his enthusiasm into reality.

Rothschilds tended to go in for variety in the exteriors of their houses. At Mentmore Baron Meyer copied an Elizabethan mansion – Wollaton Hall, near Nottingham – down to the smallest detail. At Ascott Baron Leopold built a half-timbered 'cottage', with forty bedrooms. At Halton Baron Alfred introduced touches of the baroque and the French *dix-huitième*. But inside, all their houses had a strong similarity, so much so that the phrase '*le goût* Rothschild' was coined to describe it. The 'Rothschild taste' was pioneered by Baron Meyer at Mentmore in the 1850s. By the end of the nineteenth century it was being copied by opulent financiers all over the world. They were seldom successful; really to come off *le goût* Rothschild needed not only an enormous amount of money but also an intimate knowledge of the art market.

Rothschild taste reached its climax in the interiors of Waddesdon. They were twenty-five years later than the interiors of Mentmore, and in the interval, while Rothschild taste had not changed, it had become more discriminating. The contents of Mentmore have gone for ever, dispersed in 1977 owing to the government's refusal to accept them in lieu of death duties. The collections at Halton, Tring and Aston Clinton were broken up long ago. That at Ascott survives, and also belongs to the National Trust; but the contents of Waddesdon are far more extraordinary and abundant.

Victorian Rothschilds preferred old things to new, and elaborate things to simple ones. Look where you will in their houses, it is very hard to find a plain object. They were also incurable collectors. They liked not just beautiful objects but beautiful objects by the gross. Where an ordinary millionaire would content himself with five Louis-Quinze snuffboxes, a Rothschild would have five hundred. Both tastes encouraged them to specialize in French art of the eighteenth century. At no other period have so many exquisitely finished and lavishly ornamented objects been produced. Furniture, porcelain, carpets, tapestries, bronzes, snuffboxes and clocks poured out of the French workshops to fill the salons and bedrooms of French kings, their mistresses and their courtiers. The

One of a pair of French ormolu candelabra of about 1760 in the tower drawing-room. A mixture of French panelling, furniture, *objets d'art* and full-length English portraits makes up the major part of the house's amazing contents.

Sparkling crystal combines with cool pinkish-grey marble to make the dining-room the prettiest room in the house. The splendid mirror of about 1735 came from the Hôtel de Villars in Paris.

French revolution and the troubled years that followed it released a flood of this treasure on to the market. It was eagerly bid for by collectors, but none bid bigger or better than the Rothschilds. By the end of the nineteenth century an impressive amount of what had been in French palaces and in the great eighteenth-century mansions of Paris had found its way into their houses.

So had an impressive amount of other objects. At Waddesdon by no means everything is French. Baron Ferdinand had a taste for lavish full-length portraits by Reynolds, Gainsborough, Romney and Lawrence. He owned twelve Guardis, including the two largest known examples in the world. He collected Chinese vases and German baroque china and jewellery. His important collection of late medieval and Renaissance works of art was left to the British Museum at his death; but the hole it left at Waddesdon was more than filled by collections made or inherited by his sister and his great-nephew, who owned Waddesdon after him. One could stock several country houses and an assortment of museums out of the contents of Waddesdon. In order to display them the National Trust have turned most of the upstairs bedrooms and galleries into museum rooms. Here one can see (among much else) a remarkable collection of eighteenth- and nineteenth-century buttons; a selection from the Waddesdon collection of lace and silver toys (it was typical of the Rothschilds that they collected *silver* toys); and some of the hundreds of Staffordshire and Nottingham jugs and figures that used to be in the dairy at the Home Farm at Waddesdon. A former bedroom in one of the round towers is now lined with shelves of dazzling blue Sèvres porcelain; in the middle hangs an eighteenth-century Swiss bird-cage, in which (when it is set working) a mechanical bird sings to the accompaniment of a miniature organ and a revolving glass fountain. Rothschilds were always intrigued by ingenious mechanical toys, especially when they combined exquisite craftsmanship with precious materials.

In spite of everything else, however, it is the French eighteenth century which dominates Waddesdon. The architectural design of the rooms is mostly French in character; sometimes it actually *is* French, for many of the Waddesdon interiors are lined with exquisitely carved panelling removed from eighteenth-century houses in and around Paris. And room after room is filled with French furniture and works of art. It may be hard to envisage owning or living with these costly and exquisite objects, but their craftsmanship and stylishness is dazzling. A piece of luxury French furniture was the result of two and sometimes three sets of craftsmen working in perfect unison. Not only did the skeleton have to be constructed of carefully shaped and curved wood, but it then had to be covered with a richly patterned skin made of hundreds of pieces of different exotic woods used as veneer and inlay. This wooden basis was combined with delicately worked fittings of gilded metal used for handles, key-holes and rails and to emphasize the main lines of the furniture. In a particular type of French furniture, of which there are several examples at Waddesdon, wood and metal

below left Boucher's portrait of the two-year-old Louis-Phillipe d'Orleans, Duc de Montpensier. He grew up to join the French revolutionaries and to vote for the execution of his cousin Louis XVI – only to die on the guillotine himself in 1793.

below The craftsmanship of eighteenth-century French furniture has never been surpassed. This is a detail of a roll-top desk made in 1774 by the renowned J.H.Riesener for the Comte de Provence, who became Louis XVIII of France.

This elephant vase of 1757 is one of the most decorative pieces of French porcelain at Waddesdon. Elephant vases were amongst the most prized products of the royal factory at Sèvres and came in three sizes, of which this example is the largest.

were combined with panels of white Sèvres porcelain gaily decorated with bunches or garlands of flowers.

The French furniture at Waddesdon ranges from delicate tables designed for Marie Antoinette's boudoir to showpieces on the grand scale. The icing on their cake, so to speak, comes in the form of clocks, vases, statuettes and other precious objects, all exquisite, and almost jostling each other on tabletops, mantelpieces or shelves. But of all the luxurious objects at Waddesdon perhaps none are more so than the series of sumptuous Savonnerie carpets, two of them originally made for the Louvre palace in the time of Louis XIV. And if one was to pick out one particular thing to capture the identity of the house it would be the ticking of dozens of clocks – bronze clocks, marble clocks, china clocks, clocks set with diamonds, clocks supported by golden cherubs, or with figures of gods, nymphs and goddesses reclining over them, all ticking gently away at different paces and with different accents.

left Like all the rooms at Waddesdon the morning room is crowded with objects, most of them priceless. The full-length picture over the fireplace is by Reynolds, and shows the Athenian courtesan Thais who urged Alexander the Great to burn the Persian royal palace at Persepolis. Emily Pott, a high-class prostitute of Reynolds's day, modelled for the figure of Thais.

Baron Ferdinand, like other Rothschilds of the later generations, had largely detached himself from the Rothschild banks, except as places through which to invest his money. He was able to devote his life to sport, politics, philanthropy and pleasure. Like all Rothschilds he entertained lavishly. Waddesdon was meant for use, not just as a repository for treasures. Edward VII, who had a fondness for Rothschilds, came there frequently, and once fell down the staircase. Victoria was there for the day in 1890; her visit was something of a triumph for she was much less partial to Rothschilds than her son, and Waddesdon was the only Rothschild house she ever visited.

The huge house-parties which sat down in the marble dining-room at Waddesdon could be sure of far more delicious food than was normally found in country houses of the time – even though the baron himself suffered from dyspepsia and lived largely on toast. The entertainments provided for guests included music from the baron's small private orchestra and a visit to his menagerie and aviary. The baron used to call in there most mornings to feed his ostriches. The pheasant shoots at Waddesdon were famous; every Christmas the baron and his cousin and brother-in-law Leo de Rothschild used to present every bus driver and conductor in central London with a brace of pheasants. In return they decorated their buses for the season with blue and white ribbons – the Rothschild racing colours.

It is easy to envisage house-parties at Waddesdon. It is harder to think of children playing there, or, in general, to envisage a Rothschild nursery. Indeed there never was a nursery at Waddesdon. When Baron Ferdinand died in 1898 (he caught a chill on one of his regular visits to the grave of his wife) he left Waddesdon to his sister Alice, who never married. When she died in 1922 she left it to a French Rothschild, her great-nephew James. James de Rothschild was married but had no children. It was he, on his death in 1957, who left the house, all its contents and an endowment, to the National Trust – a legacy of almost unequalled munificence.

End March–October: *House and Grounds* Wednesday–Sunday 2–6, Bank Holidays 11–6; *Grounds* Sunday 11.30–6. Closed on Wednesdays after Bank Holidays. Tea room.

Hughenden Manor
Buckinghamshire

Disraeli's Hughenden and Ferdinand de Rothschild's Waddesdon make a curious contrast. Superficially they have much in common. They are only a few miles away from each other and were built (or in the case of Hughenden remodelled) in the same twenty years. Their owners were friends, both Jewish, both married but childless. Both houses are 'manors'. They are both built on hilltops, with splendid views.

In fact, however, they are completely different. They make a good pair for a day's outing – as long as Waddesdon is visited first. The treasures of Waddesdon are superb, but there are so many of them that only the most dedicated country house visitor can leave the place without feeling stunned. At Hughenden there are no treasures at all. Several museums could be stocked out of Waddesdon, but most of the contents of Hughenden look as though they had just been picked up in London's Portobello Market. After Waddesdon, though, it is delightfully undemanding. It is a relaxing, unpretentious kind of place. The houses of dead great people, piously stuffed with neatly labelled relics, can be a bit of a bore. Hughenden is full of relics, but it is neither a boring nor a dead house. It has a personality.

The atmosphere – or lack of it – that one finds in houses is an odd thing; it is often hard to define what produces it. Some people have houses that exactly

preceding page Looking along the garden front of Hughenden Manor. Benjamin Disraeli, not yet prime minister, bought Hughenden in 1848, and remodelled the exterior in 1862–3. He used often to pace up and down in the sun along the sheltered garden terrace. *inset* Benjamin Disraeli, Earl of Beaconsfield, prime minister in 1868 and 1874–80. A detail from the portrait by Millais.

right A posthumous portrait of Disraeli's wife Mary Anne hangs over the fireplace in the drawing-room. It is based on an earlier miniature. She was a comfortably-off widow, twelve years older than Disraeli; he first made advances to her for her money but grew to love her devotedly.

left Disraeli worked and wrote his novels in this agreeable and unassuming study on the first floor. Pictures of his father and mother hang over the fireplace; the chair at the writing-table was made for him nearby in High Wycombe.

reflect their personalities; some people, often with very strong personalities, seem to have no relationship to their houses at all. Disraeli was an amazing person, but nobody could call Hughenden an amazing house. Yet it has something about it not quite like other country houses.

Whatever he was, Disraeli was not a conventional country house owner. He was almost the last person who might have been expected to become the leader of the Tories. In early Victorian days the Conservative party was the country gentleman's party. The typical Tory MP was a Church of England squire, with a country house of his own, a string of ancestors, and an estate of several thousand acres. To lead the party it was considered essential to be a peer or the son of a peer, or at the very least a baronet. Disraeli was none of these things. When he first tried to get into politics Tory country gentlemen thought him a bounder and a bit of a crook. What, they asked, did this conceited and affected young puppy with ringed fingers, curled hair, brightly striped socks, and waistcoats as flowery as his conversation, think he was up to? He was heavily in debt and believed to be not quite straight about money. He didn't hunt or shoot. Worst of all, the fellow actually wrote novels.

After four unsuccessful attempts, Disraeli finally got into parliament in 1837 as member for Maidstone. His first speech was a disaster. His manner was so ridiculously affected that the whole House of Commons burst into roars of laughter. Fourteen years later he was the leader of the Conservative party.

Disraeli succeeded for a number of reasons. He was much brighter than all the available Tory peers and landowners; on the other hand he was fascinated by their life-style and traditions, and genuinely believed that a powerful land-owning aristocracy was the best defence against too much government and too many bureaucrats. As a result he was able to make the Tories seem glamorous to themselves and to other people. Moreover, as the years went on he gradually dropped his more irritating mannerisms. He became a mysterious, sphinx-like figure with a face like a carved mask; no one knew quite what was going on behind it.

By the mid 1840s it was clear to Disraeli and everyone else that he was in the running for the leadership of the party. It was still, however, considered impossible for the party to be led by someone without a country house and estate. Disraeli not only didn't have the money to buy one, his debts (the legacy of his irresponsible youth) amounted in modern terms to about £200,000. Although he had married a wife with a comfortable income she had no capital. The situation seemed hopeless until three Tory brothers, the sons of the Duke of Portland, put up the necessary money, and enabled Disraeli to buy the Hughenden estate in 1845. For his purposes it was ideal: beautifully situated high up in the Chilterns, big enough for his political ambitions but not too big for his income, surrounded by an estate of seven hundred and fifty acres, and neither too near nor too far from London.

Disraeli loved Hughenden. Perhaps that is why it is still a nice place to be. It was his symbol of success and his bolt-hole from political life in London. What money he or his wife had to spare went on improving it. When he acquired it it was a plain white stucco house, mainly dating from the late eighteenth century. In 1862 he brought in Edward Buckton Lamb (an architect much patronized by Tory gentlemen) to make it gothic. Disraeli fondly imagined that it was 'restored to what it was before the Civil War', but nowadays it looks totally and comfortably Victorian. Outside Lamb faced it with red brick with a profusion of curiously knobbly (but not unattractive) brick arches and pinnacles. Inside he put in vaguely gothic ceilings and a few marble chimney-pieces – nothing at all elaborate because there wasn't the money for it. The furniture was very Victorian and equally unpretentious – apart from a piece or two like the florid side-table, inlaid with

The drawing-room is a charming early Victorian room, with windows opening directly on to the garden terrace.

porcelain plaques, in the drawing-room. Disraeli's wife Mary Anne embroidered some of the chair covers and probably chose most of the drawing-room furniture. Her portrait hangs over the chimney-piece.

Hughenden probably owes as much to her as to her husband. Disraeli's marriage is one of the nicest things about him. When he married her, Mary Anne was an apparently rich and rather ridiculous widow twelve years older than he was (and too old to have children). She was too flirtatious for her age and never stopped talking for a minute. Disraeli later admitted that he started making up to her for her money. He needed a rich wife and was unaware that her income was only hers for life. He became a devoted husband, however, saw through her absurdities to her love and loyalty, and came to rely on her absolutely. One of the most touching relics at Hughenden, hanging on a wall in the hall, is one side of the coach in which Disraeli used to drive to the House of Commons. One day he was driving there with his wife to make an important speech, and Mary Anne crushed her thumb in the door when she was shutting it. She sat in agony all the way to Westminster, but never said a word for fear the accident would spoil his speech. It is sad that she died in 1872, before his second and much his most successful session as prime minister.

below The library was one of Disraeli's favourite rooms. 'When I come down to Hughenden', he wrote, 'I pass the first week in sauntering about my park and examining all the trees, and then I saunter in the library and survey the books.'

The drawing-room at Hughenden reflects her taste; the dining-room is a darker and heavier room, in the approved Victorian fashion, a room for after-dinner port and family prayers. Disraeli's particular haunts were the book-lined library and the little study on the first floor. The latter is a totally unassuming and rather snug room hung with watercolours of his family; the armchair was made for him down the road in High Wycombe.

The Disraelis spent all the time they could at Hughenden. Politics were leisurely in Victorian days; there was no autumn session, and no need to go to London from the end of August until after Christmas. Disraeli usually arrived exhausted after the summer's politics, and needed a month or more to recuperate. He strolled up and down the terrace in front of the house, communing with his peacocks; went to see the two swans Hero and Leander on the little lake by the church; walked through the woods on his own or accompanied by Mary Anne in a little pony cart; and sat in the library reading in a desultory way or, as he put it, 'watching the sunbeams on the bindings of the books'.

Later he would begin to come to life again and sharpen his claws for his next political scrap with Gladstone, whom he disliked as much as Gladstone disliked him. Documents and work would start to come from London, especially during his two terms as prime minister, in 1868 and 1874–80. Every now and then he sat down and wrote another novel in his study – the only prime minister ever to do so. Politicians and friends came to stay or be entertained in considerable numbers. Mrs Disraeli had the reputation in the neighbourhood of being a close housekeeper; it was said that on one occasion when some guests failed to turn up for lunch, she sent the joint back to the butcher and asked for a refund.

In the course of his career the house gradually filled up with presents and mementoes. Disraeli hung the hall and corridor with what he called his 'Gallery of Friendship' – portraits of all the people he had known best during his long life. Caricatures of himself and fellow politicians gradually accumulated. Many people sent presents, including Queen Victoria. Bronze statuettes of her seated at her spinning-wheel, and of her beloved Scottish servant John Brown, are prominent features of the drawing-room and dining-room. She gave them to Disraeli in the year of his retirement from politics in 1880.

All his life Disraeli had the knack of chatting up elderly ladies, and he was never more successful than with the queen. Gladstone talked to her like a public meeting; Disraeli flattered her, confided in her, and made her laugh. He was her favourite prime minister; she made him Earl of Beaconsfield, and paid him the rare compliment of coming to lunch with him at Hughenden in 1877 to demonstrate her support when politically he was going through a bad period. She wanted to visit him in his final illness, but Disraeli, who had an excellent sense of humour to the end, said, 'No, it is better not. She would only ask me to take a message to Albert.' He died at Hughenden in 1881 and was buried in the churchyard. The queen sent a wreath of primroses with the inscription: 'His favourite flower from Osborne, a tribute of affection from Queen Victoria.'

below left This amazing mid-Victorian side-table inlaid with plaques of Dresden china, is the most elaborate but perhaps not the most beautiful piece of furniture in the house.

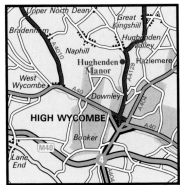

March–November: Wednesday–Friday 2–6, weekends and Bank Holidays 12.30–6. Closed Good Friday. Tea available March–October weekends and Bank Holidays.

Bateman's
Sussex

Bateman's
Sussex

Kipling first came to know Sussex at Rottingdean. His uncle, the painter Edward Burne-Jones, and numerous other relatives had houses there; the Kiplings came to join them in 1897. It was of Rottingdean and 'Sussex by the sea' that he was thinking when he wrote:

> God gives all men all earth to love
> But since man's heart is small,
> Ordains for each one spot shall prove
> Beloved over all.

But tourists from Brighton began to spoil the quiet village for him, and in 1902 he moved inland and bought Bateman's, near the little village of Burwash, deep in the Sussex Weald.

The Weald used to be almost entirely covered by forests. This made it the main centre of the iron industry in Roman days, and again in the sixteenth and seventeenth centuries. Iron was then smelted by charcoal rather than coal; bit by bit the Wealden forest disappeared as the trees were cut down for charcoal. Many fortunes, large and small, were made by the Sussex iron-masters before the Midland coal mines were opened up and killed the Sussex industry.

There were two forges at Burwash and the owner of one of them built Bateman's in 1634. He built a quiet gabled manor-house, as English as the meadows and woods surrounding it. The main walls are of rich grey-yellow stone, but the tall hospitable chimney-stacks are of mellowed brick; the windows have gothic mouldings, and only a touch of ornament here and there suggests the new Italian fashions that were sweeping through London and the houses of the great.

The house later became a farmhouse, like many other iron-master's houses; one wing was demolished, but otherwise it was left almost unaltered. Two oast-houses were built next to the farmhouse in about 1770. Kipling described it shortly after he bought it: 'a grey stone lichened house – AD 1634 over the door – beamed, panelled, with an old oak staircase, and all untouched and unfaked . . . It is a good and peaceable place standing in terraced lawns nigh to a walled garden of old red brick, and two fat-headed oast-houses with red brick stomachs, and an aged silver-grey dovecot on top.' One of his family said that 'the house stands like a beautiful cup on a saucer to match'.

At Bateman's Kipling claimed that he and his wife 'discovered England, which we had never done before'. Buying it was the starting-point of a new phase in his writing. The Kipling of the Indian stories and the *Barrack Room Ballads* gave way to the Kipling of *Puck of Pook's Hill* and *Rewards and Fairies*. These and other books were written for his two children and many incidents in them were based on the traditions and countryside round Bateman's.

Much as Kipling loved Sussex, however, he was also the man who wrote 'The Ship That Found Herself' and shocked his arty contemporaries by his enthusiasm for huge engines and smoothly-working machinery. He loved the old buildings of Sussex but had no desire to live by candlelight or travel by pony-cart. He was an enthusiastic motorist in the pioneering days of motoring. He first discovered Bateman's when chuffing down the steep hill from Burwash in a 'locomobile' – one of the short-lived race of steam-driven cars. A year or two later he bought a Lanchester; the motoring world was so small in those days that the car was personally delivered to him by Mr Lanchester himself. The property at Bateman's

preceding page Bateman's lies cupped in a shallow valley below the village of Burwash. The gabled wing on the left was originally matched by one on the right, which was probably demolished when the house became a farmhouse in the eighteenth century. The tile-hung oast-houses were built in about 1770.
inset Rudyard Kipling (1865–1936). A detail from a portrait by Philip Burne-Jones.

right Looking across the garden pond to the house. Built in the 1630s by a Sussex iron-master, it was bought by Rudyard Kipling in 1902. He described it as 'a good and peaceable place'.

included an old watermill, four hundred yards from the house on the little River Dudwell. Kipling took out the waterwheel and replaced it with a water turbine and an electric generator, which supplied electricity to the house. The turbine has now become a museum piece and has been lovingly restored; but in its day it was extremely up to date. Even the great pool which the Kiplings installed to the south of the house, in a traditional setting of statues and clipped yew hedges, had an up-to-date concrete bottom to make it more convenient for swimming and boating. The cryptic initials F.I.P., scrawled by Kipling after names in the Bateman's visitors' book, stand for 'fell in pool' – something that seems to have happened very often.

A great many visitors came to Bateman's for a meal or to spend the night. Some were world-famous, many were unknown young writers to whom Kipling gave help and advice. A visit to Bateman's had its hazards however. Kipling's American wife saw her job in life as keeping her husband free from worry and interruptions; unlike her husband she was often far from welcoming to visitors. Neither of the Kiplings had any feeling for comfort; the chairs were hard and the house very cold in winter, in spite of the huge log fire blazing in the hall where the Kiplings always had tea. The rooms are panelled and rather dark. The contents are mainly seventeenth century – old oak furniture, a few pieces of tapestry and some fine clocks. As Kipling's daughter put it, 'many of the things were beautiful in themselves, but the whole effect was rather sparse'.

The guest-room upstairs has been converted into a museum. It is full of Kipling

above In the panelled hall the Kiplings and their friends used to have tea before a blazing log fire. Objects from Tibet on the oak credence chest to the left are a reminder of Kipling's early years in the East.

right The study, facing east and south from the first floor, has been left much as it was when Kipling died in 1936 – down to the typewriter which he began to use shortly before his death.

documents and relics, including old Indian Railway paperbacks of his early stories, and some pages of advice to his son on first going to school ('If you are going to steal apples, steal them on a Sunday, when you can hide them in your top hat'). But much the most personal room is, and probably always was, Kipling's book-lined study at the top of the old oak stairs. It is crowded with curiosities: old carved ivory, daggers, a pipe carved with the head of Queen Victoria, some pieces from the bunting of Nelson's *Victory*, an ironwork pencase like the lama's pencase in *Kim*. A big model of a man-of-war reminds one of Kipling's lifelong admiration for the beauty of sailing-ships. But essentially it is a work room. The capacious inkstained writing-table is still scattered with Kipling's pen-wipers and pipe-cleaners, and the little furry seal which he used as a paperweight. He wrote on large pads of pale blue paper especially made for him, frequently crossing out and tossing rejected sheets into a huge waste-paper basket. Towards the end of his life he started to use the old-fashioned typewriter which still stands on the writing desk. In between writing he spent many hours lying full length on the extremely hard sofa, working out his ideas. When he was writing poetry he would stride up and down, humming a tune and fitting the words to it.

Kipling died in 1936 and was buried in Westminster Abbey. When Mrs Kipling died three years later she left Bateman's and its contents to the National Trust as a memorial to him.

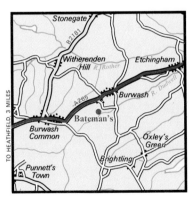

March–October: daily (except Friday) 2–6. June–September: Monday–Thursday 11–12.30. Good Friday 2–6. No dogs. Teashop.

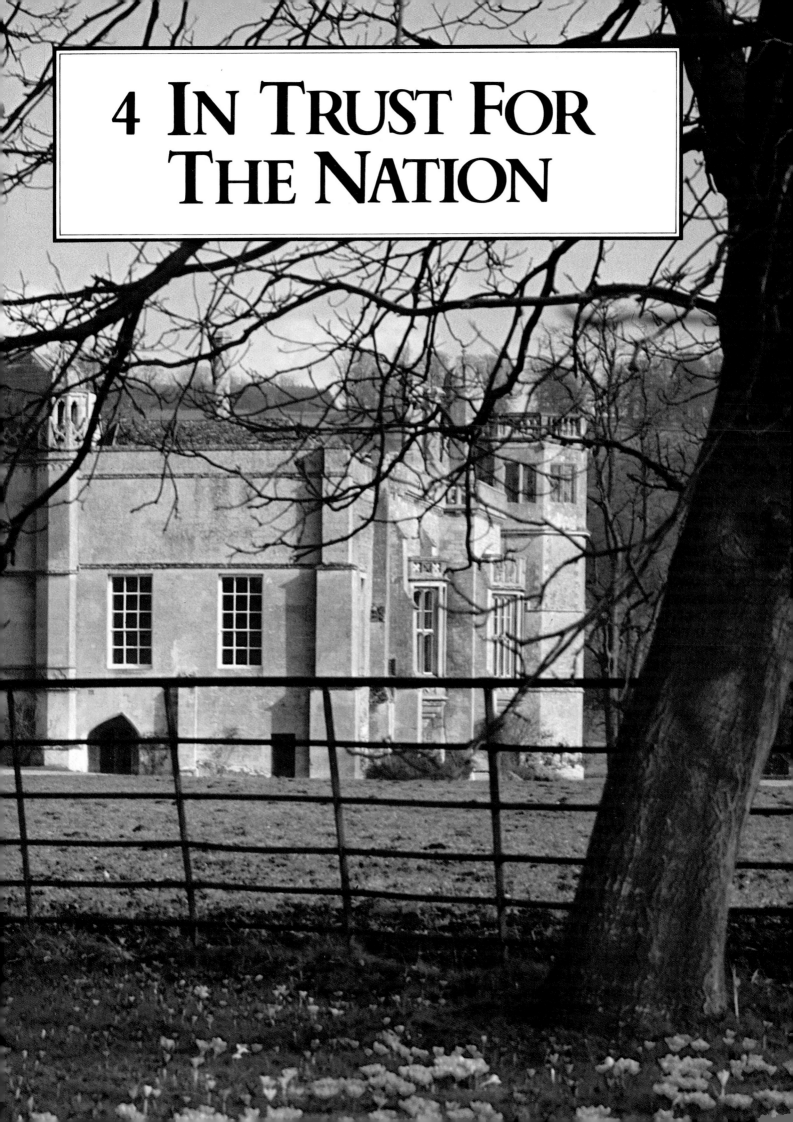

4 In Trust For The Nation

Lacock Abbey
Wiltshire

Lacock is one of the most interesting of a remarkable group of country houses – those made out of the monastic buildings closed down by Henry VIII. Between 1536 and 1540 Henry closed all the religious houses in England. Their buildings and their vast estates were taken over by the crown, and in the years that followed more and more of these church lands and buildings were sold by Henry and his successors (often at knock-down prices), or went as reward or payment to courtiers, government officials or powerful people.

Very often the people who acquired a convent or a monastery moved into the buildings and made a house of them. The way in which this was done varied from place to place. Some adapted the actual church as part of their house. When John Fleetwood acquired Calwich Abbey in Staffordshire in the 1540s it was said that he made 'a parlour of the chancel, a hall of the church and a kitchen of the steeple'. At Buckland Abbey in Devon one can see what is still quite clearly a church by origin, which has had a house inserted in it. But other new owners pulled the church down, either because it was inconvenient to convert or because they were afraid of sacrilege. In that case they concentrated on the other monastic buildings.

When the owners first moved in they usually made fairly minor alterations – just enough to produce a habitable house. Very often the lodgings of the abbot or prioress were quite adequate for their purposes, as by the end of the Middle Ages heads of religious houses tended to do themselves rather well. But in the course of time more and more of the original monastic buildings disappeared as a result of rebuilding and alterations over the generations. Longleat was originally a monastic house, acquired by Sir John Thynne in 1541; but by the seventeenth century almost every vestige of the original buildings had disappeared, except for the shape of one courtyard which marked the site of the cloister.

Lacock had a quite different development, however, which is why it is so interesting. It was originally a convent, founded in 1232 – a rather select and extremely well-run convent, which because of its good reputation was one of the last of the religious houses to be dissolved. In 1539 the convent and its lands were sold for £783 to Sir William Sharington, who had a job at court and a good connection there. Sharington pulled down the church and added a new courtyard to the other side of the convent buildings. He moved in upstairs in the main building, and left everything downstairs almost untouched. His successors altered and added upstairs, but also did very little down below.

The result is that from the outside Lacock looks like a rambling country house of many dates, with nothing in the least reminiscent of religion about it. But if one goes through any of the ground-floor doors one is transported into a different world. The country house turns into a medieval convent, less altered than almost any medieval religious building in England. Leading off an untouched cloister, roofed by an exquisitely graceful fan vault of the fifteenth century, are a series of earlier vaulted rooms. The stately chapter house and refectory are still there; so is the little room which belonged to the nuns' chaplain, and the parlour where they talked to visitors from outside; so is the calefactory or warming-room, which contained the only fireplace accessible to the nuns, who were allowed to resort there at certain times during the winter. Upstairs, however, one is back in the world of the English country house. Remains of the convent can be found upstairs too, but they are all hidden from view, above ceilings or in back passages.

Why did Sharington abandon the ground floor in this way? Was it because he had the sensitivity not to spoil the vaulted rooms and cloisters? Or was it just for

top W.H.Fox Talbot, owner of Lacock Abbey in the nineteenth century and pioneer of photography.

above An oriel window in the south gallery, from a photograph taken by W.H.Fox Talbot in 1835. The negative is in the Science Museum in South Kensington, and is the oldest surviving negative in the world. It is about the size of a postage stamp.

preceding pages The west front of Lacock Abbey. The gothic hall is behind the two large windows in the centre.

Looking across the River Avon to the south and east fronts of Lacock. The oriel windows of the south gallery can be seen on the left. The gothic windows along the ground floor to the right light some of the rooms used by the Augustinian nuns, whose abbey Lacock was until they were expelled in 1539. Their quarters survive almost unaltered on the ground floor; everything above was built by Sir William Sharington and subsequent owners.

convenience because the downstairs rooms were awkward to convert, and by using them for cellars, storage and servants he got comfortably dry quarters for himself upstairs? We shall never be certain. Two things are known about Sharington, and one can make what one wants of them: he was a crook, and he had exquisite taste.

There is no doubt about his crookedness. In 1546 he was appointed vice-treasurer of the Bristol Mint. He made a great deal of money for himself by 'clipping the coinage' – actually clipping off the edges of coins and re-smelting the clippings, while the remains of the original coin, which bore the mint's impression, were returned to circulation. He used the proceeds to subsidize his friend Thomas Seymour, Lord Seymour of Sudeley. Seymour was plotting against the government and Sharington joined in his plots. Both of them were arrested in 1549. Sharington turned king's evidence and put all the blame on Seymour. Seymour was beheaded, but Sharington escaped with a prison sentence and the loss of his property. Later he was pardoned and got everything back on payment of a fine of £800.

His taste is equally undeniable; one only has to look around Lacock to see the evidence of it. Much of what he did has been destroyed, but everything that remains is not only exquisite but has a very personal quality. When he built, new

Renaissance fashions in ornament were just beginning to seep into England. Many builders at the time used these in an ignorant and clumsy way. Sharington used them skilfully but he also had a feeling for the gothic style and ornament which, in the long run, the Renaissance was going to drive out. He combined the two together in a highly personal and completely successful manner. Everything he did was delicate. His slender, fluted and twisted chimney-stacks which run along the east front are basically gothic, although even some of them have little Renaissance balusters incorporated in them. His stable yard looks completely traditional and medieval until one notices that everywhere Sharington has introduced little Renaissance 'consoles' or scrolls, a favourite motif of his. A chimney-piece in the stone gallery, on the other hand, is completely of the Renaissance at its most delicate.

The most remarkable and beautiful survival of Sharington, however, is the octagonal tower which he added to the south-east corner of the building. It is four storeys high, capped by a little cupola and a Renaissance balustrade. The top floor, which rises above the roof line, is approached by a narrow stone walk guarded by a parapet. It is a pleasant place from which to survey the landscape; and Sharington probably planned it as a place to take exercise, as well as a means of access to the room in the tower.

The top room was planned as a miniature banqueting room, and the room below as a strong-room and possibly as a study. The main feature of each room is an octagonal stone table with marble top, placed exactly in the centre. Both tables are beautifully carved with figures and ornament in the full manner of the Renaissance. The carver of these and other details at Lacock was probably John Chapman, who had worked for Henry VIII. The upper room is not open to visitors (except on special application) but the lower room is. It has an iron-plated door and a curiously vaulted roof decorated with carvings of the scorpion, which was Sharington's crest. The table is supported by four fauns holding bunches of

below left A carved stone table of about 1550 in Sir William Sharington's strongroom in the tower.

below The parapet walk along the top of the south front leads to the higher of the two rooms in Sharington's tower.

fruit above their heads. In the walls are recesses for documents, books and papers. The room is rather dark and very small. It is an extraordinary and mysterious place.

Sharington had no children. Lacock was inherited by his brother Henry who only had two daughters. Olive Sharington, the eldest of these and his heiress, married John Talbot. The story of their marriage is related by John Aubrey, the seventeenth-century antiquarian, who knew their grandson. Henry Sharington had forbidden the marriage. Olive was standing on the roof walk talking to her disconsolate lover in the garden far below. 'Oh, that I could jump into your arms,' sighed the loving girl. 'I would catch you, my darling,' said her lover, obviously not meaning to be taken seriously. Olive immediately leapt over the parapet. Her dress flared out like a parachute and slightly broke her fall, otherwise she would no doubt have killed both herself and her lover, into whose arms she fell. As it was he was so badly winded as to seem dead, but he recovered. Henry Sharington allowed them to marry after that; he said they had earned it.

The next important person in the story of Lacock is John Ivory Talbot, who owned it for sixty years in the eighteenth century. It was he who replaced Sharington's hall with the gothic hall by which the house is now entered. He made many other changes in the house as well, to bring it up to Georgian standards of convenience and comfort. To begin with, his redecorations were in the classical style; the most important room of this kind to survive is the dining-room. But the reign of the classical portico and pediment, although by no means over, was ceasing to be absolute. Gothic was coming back into fashion again, especially for houses which had ancient associations, like Lacock. So John Ivory Talbot determined to build a gothic hall. He went to his friend Sanderson Miller for designs. Miller was a country gentleman who was also (as many country gentlemen were in those days) an amateur architect; he specialized in gothic. But there was still no real understanding of medieval gothic. Miller's hall has little

below The hall was redecorated in 1754–5 in a revived version of the gothic style.

below right The blue parlour is lined with portraits and early eighteenth-century panelling. On the floor is an Aubusson carpet over a hundred years old.

left The nuns' rooms are grouped round the exquisite fifteenth-century cloister, one of the finest surviving examples of perpendicular gothic fan-vaulting in England. Its south walk ran along the abbey church, which Sir William Sharington demolished.

right The warming-room dates from the thirteenth century, and is the only room in which the nuns had access to a fire. The huge iron cauldron dates from 1500 and probably once stood in the nuns' kitchen.

End March–October: Wednesday–Sunday and Bank Holidays 2–6. June–September: daily 2–6. November–March: societies admitted by arrangement.

relationship to anything put up in the Middle Ages, but it is very charming none the less. Inside it is plastered to imitate stone, and surrounded by niches filled with terracotta statues made by a travelling Austrian called Sederbach. Sederbach's statues are even less gothic than the hall; they are pure rococo, full of the swirling life and movement which makes continental churches of this period so exciting. The ceiling is covered with the coats of arms of Talbot's friends. The hall was opened with a great dinner in 1755. Talbot wrote to Miller, 'All my friends who are in the country, and whose arms are emblazoned on the ceiling, will do me the honour of their company, and a grand sacrifice to Bacchus will be the consequence.'

The last important alterations to Lacock were made in the nineteenth century. They include the formation of the south gallery, the oriel windows of which figure prominently on the south front. Lacock is famous all over the world because of the man who built them: William Henry Fox Talbot, who shares with Daguerre the credit for inventing photography. He started experimenting in the 1830s. Hanging by one of the oriel windows in the south gallery is a little blurred photograph of the window itself. It is not something at which one would normally give a second glance; but in fact it is a print from the oldest negative in existence in the world, made in 1835.

Lacock Abbey and village were given to the National Trust in 1944 by Fox Talbot's granddaughter Miss Matilda Talbot (a redoubtable character in her own right). Her great-nephew and niece still live in part of the Abbey. A museum illustrating Fox Talbot's career and achievements was opened in 1975 in a converted barn by the Abbey gates. He was a botanist, mathematician, astronomer and Egyptologist, as well as a pioneer of photography. One of the pay-offs of the country-house system was that its revenues provided the money and leisure to enable a clever man to follow his own bent. Fox Talbot is one of the most eminent of a group of country-house scientists who researched and experimented in their outbuildings or attics, and then produced results which startled the world.

Cotehele
Cornwall

Cotehele is often described as a house which has scarcely been altered since it was built in the years around 1500. That is true enough of its architecture, but untrue of almost everything else – especially of its setting. All the soft lushness of South Cornish lawns, trees and vegetation cushion it from the outside world. Long romantic drives and walks lead up to it through the woods from the broad and peaceful valley of the Tamar. There are more lawns in its main courtyard, and creepers grow in profusion up its mellow walls.

Originally it looked very different, however. Sir Richard Edgcumbe, who started to build Cotehele in the 1480s, was a tough professional soldier living in a tough part of the world, and he built a tough house. There was little or no law in Cornwall in the fifteenth century; people had to look after themselves. In the 1470s Richard Edgcumbe had a blood feud with his neighbour Robert Willoughby of Bere Ferrers which involved ambush, assault and attempts to murder Edgcumbe and burn down Cotehele. In 1483 he joined the Duke of Buckingham in a revolt against Richard III (Buckingham claimed he had a better right to the throne than Richard). The revolt was a fiasco, and Edgcumbe was in danger of his life. Sir Henry Bodrugan, who represented the king in Cornwall, besieged him in Cotehele. Edgcumbe managed to break through the cordon, and ran down through the woods to the river, pursued by his enemies. At the water's edge he acted with great presence of mind: he hid in the bushes, put a stone into his hat, and threw it into the water; his pursuers saw it floating down the river and concluded that he was drowned.

Edgcumbe escaped to France where he joined Henry Tudor. In the end that made his fortune. In 1485 Henry defeated Richard III at the Battle of Bosworth and became Henry VII. Richard Edgcumbe was knighted, became comptroller of the king's household and was given Sir Henry Bodrugan's estates. He even had the satisfaction of getting an appropriate revenge by literally chasing his enemy into the sea. Bodrugan leapt over the cliff now known as Bodrugan's Leap near Mevagissey, and escaped to Ireland.

Richard Edgcumbe started to build the house at Cotehele in the days of his prosperity, but he built it remembering the past and taking precautions for the future. His house looked at the outside world through tiny windows cut through the thick granite, well above ground level; any big windows looked on to internal courtyards. There were already woods along the Tamar in those days,

left The battlemented gatehouse on the east front was built of Cornish granite by Sir Richard Edgcumbe in the late fifteenth century. A cobbled way leads through the archway into the main court.

right The courtyard showing the little gable over the chapel window and the larger one over the handsome Tudor windows, which light the parlour and the great chamber built by Sir Richard Edgcumbe's son Piers. To the right is one of the windows of the hall.

but for reasons of security they would not have been allowed to grow near the house. No houses at the time had big gardens; whatever they did have was almost entirely utilitarian. The surrounding countryside, before the days of fertilizers and modern methods of agriculture, was much bleaker than it is now and very thinly populated. The granite of which the house is built is almost impossible to carve, and allows for little in the way of ornament. The house must have looked strong and commanding, rather than mellow and welcoming. To those who penetrated to the courtyard it suggested gentler times, however, especially as completed by Richard's son Piers.

Richard seems to have been a natural soldier. A few years after his return to England he went off again to fight for Anne of Brittany in France, apparently as a mercenary, and he died there in 1489. His son built the hall range at Cotehele and had completed it by 1520. It was built round a second small courtyard, but the three main rooms – the hall and two rooms off it, one above the other – all have big windows looking on to the main court and butting against the traceried window of Richard's chapel. The hall is a lofty room with a fine timber roof. But the detail everywhere is very simple and has the boldly rounded mouldings that are the natural result of working in granite.

Almost the only ornamental feature on the outside of Cotehele is the charming little bell-turret on Sir Richard's chapel. One of its two bells is also the bell of a clock, and this clock is perhaps the most remarkable feature of Cotehele. It was installed in the chapel in the 1480s and is still in working order. It was constructed before the invention of the pendulum and the clockface, and is regulated by the horizontal balance known as a foliot. It is the earliest clock in England still in

The clock in the chapel dates from the 1480s. This rare survival of a pre-pendulum clock is still in sound working order.

working order in its original position; pre-pendulum clocks were almost always converted to pendulums at a later date.

The main subsequent alteration which took place at Cotehele was the addition of a tall tower to one corner in 1627. Its floors are all on a different level from those in the main block, which makes a tour of the house a curiously up and down affair. It is said to have been built by Sir Thomas Coteele, a London merchant whose daughter married an Edgcumbe and who lived at Cotehele for some years (the resemblance of the names was pure coincidence). By 1627 the Edgcumbes were living more and more at a new house which they had built down river from Cotehele in the 1550s. It looked over Plymouth Sound and was grandiloquently called Mount Edgcumbe. By the end of the seventeenth century the family had given up Cotehele almost entirely.

When going round the inside of Cotehele one needs to be gently sceptical. It is not a sleeping-beauty kind of house, where the owners moved out in 1700 and nothing has been touched since. By the end of the eighteenth century old-fashioned houses were becoming objects of curiosity. Cotehele began to be visited by tourists, or be made the object of outings by house-parties staying at Mount Edgcumbe (George III and his wife paid this kind of visit in 1789, and the cushions they sat on are still reverently preserved). Cotehele was arranged as the Edgcumbes, by now Earls of Mount Edgcumbe, thought an old-fashioned house ought to be arranged. Much of the furniture and tapestry was no doubt always at Cotehele, or at least was brought over from Mount Edgcumbe; but a good deal (it will probably never be known how much) was brought in from other sources.

above The medieval dovecot in the valley garden below the house. The pond was originally a stew pond, where fish were kept and fed until needed for eating in the house.

right The early sixteenth-century hall, as depicted in a lithograph of about 1840. It is being prepared for the annual tenants' dinner, when the Earl of Mount Edgcumbe sat in the great chair at the end of the room and entertained his farmers to a lavish banquet.

The arms, antlers and old oak chairs in the hall, for instance, are not – with a few exceptions – relics of old Cotehele, but the kind of job lot which many country house owners in search of an old-fashioned décor were picking up at London antique dealers in the early nineteenth century. At least two of the four-poster beds are not genuine Elizabethan four-posters but nineteenth-century fakes made up from bits of old carving; and even though all the tapestry is genuinely old, the way it is used almost like wallpaper is more typical of the nineteenth than of the sixteenth or seventeenth centuries. It is true that the rooms have been amazingly little altered since they were illustrated in a book on Cotehele published in about 1840; but by then the stage had already been set.

Perhaps it is best not to worry too much about the authenticity of the rooms at Cotehele, but just to surrender to their atmosphere. The dominant impression many visitors will carry away is of old beds and old tapestries in romantically dusky rooms. There is tapestry everywhere at Cotehele, often faded, jumbled together or partly blocked by furniture, so that what sticks in the mind is less an intelligible series than strange unrelated fragments – some cherubs playing, a scene in a garden, a parrot in a cage, huge figures looming out of dark corners. It is all reminiscent of Alexander Pope's couplet:

> He stares tremendous with a threatening eye
> Like some fierce tyrant in old tapestry.

Although Cotehele was little used by the Edgcumbes (except on and off as a dower house) it was still the centre of a big estate. It had its wheelwright's shop, blacksmith's forge, sawpits and cider mill at Cotehele Mill, a short walk from the house. Down by the river is Cotehele Quay, from which sailing barges and, later, steam passenger boats used to sail up and down the Tamar. Before the railway was built, as late as 1907, the river was the main means of transport, and there were quays all along it. The mill and quay at Cotehele have been restored by the National Trust and the last of the Tamar sailing barges is being re-rigged and rebuilt there. There is, in fact, much to see at Cotehele besides the house; visitors can walk for miles through the woods along the Tamar, visit the dovecot not far from the house (the lush setting of which seems to epitomize the romantic spirit of Cotehele today) and, a little further on, find the chapel above the river which Sir Richard Edgcumbe built to commemorate his escape from his enemies.

above left A bed in Queen Anne's room at the top of the tower which was added to a corner of the house in 1627.

above A seventeenth-century Flemish tapestry in the red room shows the death of Remus, one of the founders of Rome.

End March–October: *House and Garden* daily 11–6. November–March: *Garden* daily during daylight hours. Refreshments available.

Little Moreton Hall
Cheshire

Little Moreton Hall
Cheshire

In these days, when almost anything can be transported almost anywhere, it is easy to forget that this was not always the case. The way houses were built and the way they looked was heavily conditioned by where they were. Houses in an area where there was no good stone could only be built of stone at enormous expense, unless they were next door to a port or a navigable river. Otherwise the stone had to be carried by water to the nearest possible point, and then hauled by teams of oxen on wooden drags along roads that were little more than tracks. All this cost a lot of money.

Brick-making flourished in England in the days of the Romans; but when the Romans left the technique was largely forgotten, until it was gradually revived in the fifteenth century (with a few pioneers in the fourteenth). In stoneless areas the poor built their houses out of mud or clay, and the more prosperous out of wood, with an infilling of clay, straw and branches. The wooden framework was made in sections on the site out of timbers joined together horizontally and vertically by wooden pegs. The sections were hauled into position, usually on stone or rubble foundations. The spaces between the timbers were either used as doors and windows or filled with a mixture of clay and straw (known as 'daub') spread over

preceding page The south wing of Little Moreton Hall, seen across the moat. The long gallery runs behind the strip window on the top floor.

below Until the end of the sixteenth century houses in areas where there was no good building stone were normally constructed of wood. The diagram shows a timber frame with projecting upper storey or jetty, as at Little Moreton Hall.

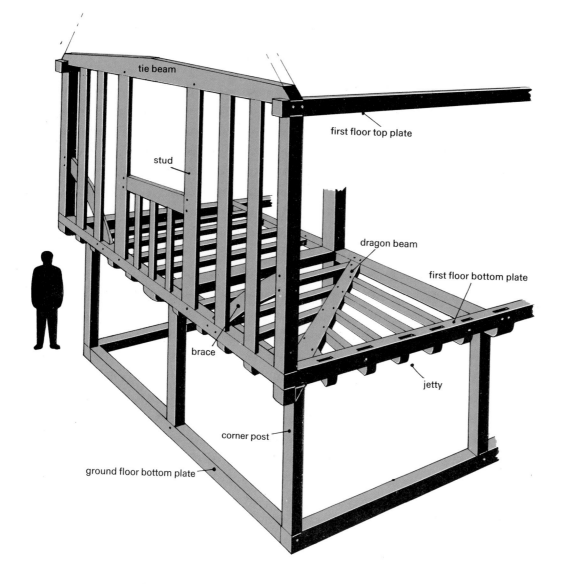

tie beam

first floor top plate

stud

dragon beam

first floor bottom plate

brace

jetty

corner post

ground floor bottom plate

The north front faces the
Elizabethan-style garden laid
out in recent years, and dates
mainly from the fifteenth
century. Sash windows were
inserted in one corner in the
eighteenth century.

a mesh of branches (known as 'wattle'). The floor area of the house could be
increased relative to the size of the foundations by projecting the upper floors over
the lower area. This was easy to do in wood, but difficult (and, beyond a foot or
so, virtually impossible) in stone.

One of the problems of timber-framed houses was what to do with the
fireplaces. If possible they were joined to chimney-stacks built of any available
stone. Failing that, houses had to rely on braziers in the smaller rooms and a
fireplace in the middle of the floor in the main hall, with the smoke escaping
through a vent in the roof. Neither system was at all satisfactory.

In the end, timber construction in England was driven out by brick. Bricks
were just as cheap, could often be made within a few hundred yards of the house,
and could not catch fire. Moreover, as more and more of the great indigenous
forests of England were cut down, timber became scarcer. The great days of the
half-timbered house came in the sixteenth and early seventeenth centuries. Brick
was then available for foundations, chimney-stacks and even as infilling between
the timbers, but had not yet superseded wood. Timber was still cheap, and glass
becoming cheaper – and there was more money around to buy it with.

The Elizabethans loved making patterns. Timber-framed houses could become
lanterns of glass-filled timber. The lead glazing bars which held together the small
panes of glass (there was still no technology for making bigger ones) could be
arranged in every kind of pattern. Smaller timbers could be used to make yet
more patterns within the main structural grid. The result was extremely
decorative and an exhilarating change for people used to living in dark and poky
houses with small windows. The Elizabethans were so delighted by the novelty of
these lantern-houses that they were prepared to put up with their lack of
insulation, and with being hot in summer and cold in winter.

Cheshire is one of the best counties in which to find half-timbered houses, and
none is better than Little Moreton Hall. Although at first sight it looks more or
less all of a piece, in fact it has a building history of well over a hundred years,

153

involving three or four generations. During all this time it belonged to the family who had been living on the site since the thirteenth century. Like many such families in the Middle Ages they had the same name as their home – they were called 'of' (or 'de') Moreton to begin with, and then just Moreton. The site was moated for security; the moat is probably a good deal older than the present building, the earliest part of which dates from the late fifteenth century. It was remodelled and extended in the 1550s, and extended again, probably in the 1570s. There were minor alterations in the seventeenth century. In the eighteenth century it was owned by Sir William Moreton, a lawyer who became recorder of London. He lived mainly in the south, but paid occasional visits to Cheshire. He put a couple of eighteenth-century fireplaces into the house and fitted one room with up-to-date sash windows. Succeeding Moretons were there less and less, and more and more bits of it were gradually rented off as a farmhouse. By the early nineteenth century there were hens pecking about on the floor of the great hall and many of the rooms were used for storing corn. The Moreton family and their

Looking down into the courtyard from the long gallery in the south wing. The amazing lantern windows were added to the earlier north wing in 1559. Richard Dale, the carpenter who constructed them, and his client William Moreton were so proud of their work that they carved their names and the date on a border below the gables.

successors kept the house in reasonable repair, however, and gave it to the National Trust in 1937. Its history explains why the house has been so little altered since the seventeenth century – and also why it has little in the way of contents, although what there is is extremely interesting.

To get some idea of what the original fifteenth-century house was like, one has to imagine the present house without the whole front portion through which one now enters it, and without the amazing bay windows which face visitors as they come into the courtyard. What is left is a typical H-shaped late medieval house with a two-storey hall in the middle, a kitchen with lodging chambers above it at one end, and a parlour and more lodgings at the other. The effect can still be seen, comparatively little altered, from the Elizabethan-style herb garden which the National Trust has made at the back of the house.

This fifteenth-century house had no chimney-stacks; the hall was warmed from a central hearth, and the whole household, including the Moretons themselves, almost certainly ate there. But in the 1550s these old-fashioned arrangements were replaced by something much more advanced. The house was owned by William Moreton about whom one wishes a little more was known. He was obviously not rich enough to employ the best craftsmen, or to build anything very grand (the Moreton property was a comparatively small one), but what he did was sufficiently up to date to suggest that he was more than a country squire. Perhaps, as often happened with the gentry of those days, he had worked in the household of a great family, and seen a bit of the world.

William Moreton took the family firmly away from the rest of the household by adding on a spacious new dining parlour lit by a huge bay window. The hall as a result became less important, and he reduced it in height by putting an upper floor in it; the space above, up in the roof, was probably used as a dormitory for servants (at a later stage the floor was taken out again, perhaps to make a barn when the house became a farm).

Two original tables stand in the hall today. The long one has probably always been in the hall; the other is probably the 'big round table' (actually it is octagonal) which, at the time an inventory was made in 1603, was standing in the bay window of the parlour. The window bay must have been a pleasant place to eat in; and in general the parlour (now shown as the drawing-room) is a very agreeable room, probably used as a combined dining- and living-room. But William Moreton's work is at its most spectacular when seen from the outside. He paired the parlour bay window by building a second one to light the hall. Both windows rise through two storeys, and to the left of them he built a new porch and inserted two more big windows. As a result the whole of this side of the courtyard seems to be bursting with wood and glass – with a zigzag of seven gables on top of them. There was only just room to squash the two bay windows in, and at first-floor level they merge into each other like Siamese twins. A carved inscription along the top of them reads: 'God is Al in Al Thing: This windous whire made by William Moreton in the yeare of Oure Lorde MDLIX. Richard Dale Carpenter made thies windous by the grac of god.' Nothing else is known about Richard Dale.

William Moreton died in 1563. He left money in his will to enable his 'chief wright' Richard Dale to complete the house. This suggests that before his death he had planned what is now the front half of the house – the gatehouse range to the south, and the half of the east courtyard range beyond the parlour. This part of the range contains a chapel. It is possible that all this may have been started in the 1560s, and perhaps finished about 1570.

An odd thing about the gatehouse range is that it seems always to have had its own kitchen. This is often explained by saying that it was a self-contained wing for guests, but this was not the Elizabethan way of doing things. It is much more likely that it was in fact a separate or semi-separate dwelling, and that in the

left The long gallery at the top of the south wing probably dates from about 1570, and undulates owing to the warping of the timbers. Such galleries were used for exercise in cold and rainy weather.

right The two tables in the great hall in the north wing have always been in the house. They probably date from the late sixteenth century, although the long table may have been altered.

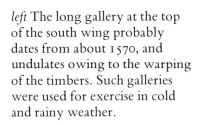

March: weekends only 2–6. April–October: daily (except Tuesday) 2–6. Parties by arrangement. Tea room.

second half of the century Little Moreton Hall was shared by two brothers, or a father and son, or a son and his widowed mother. There are quite a few examples of this arrangement in Lancashire and Cheshire houses of the period.

The gatehouse range has a handsome room on the first floor (now divided into two); but its most exciting feature is the long gallery on the second floor. It has been suggested that this was added later. There is nothing in the timber structure to support this idea, however, although it may have been an addition thought up when the wing was half-built.

Whatever its exact date, the gallery must have caused much heart-burning and gossip among the neighbouring squires when it was first put up. Inside and out it was sensational for its date and place. It is a lantern of almost continuous glass sixty-eight feet long, and seems to be balancing precariously on the roof of the structure underneath it. The Moretons, as they paced up and down it to take their winter exercise, or their children, when they played there in wet weather, must have felt they were suspended in the sky, or were bucking up and down on the bridge of a ship at sea, for the floor rises and falls owing to the warping of the timbers. It must have looked even more fragile before rather clumsy cross-timbers were inserted in the seventeenth century, to support a lower ceiling which has since been removed.

Over the windows at either end of the gallery (one of them has been filled in) are emblematic plasterwork figures with attached inscriptions, designed to show the advantages of knowledge and the dangers of ignorance. The Elizabethans were fond of incorporating propaganda for good conduct, or episodes from the Bible, into the decoration of their houses. An exciting new discovery has recently been made in the room next to the parlour. Later panelling had concealed a frieze of vivid little pictures showing the story of Daniel, with painted inscriptions and patterns surrounding them. After careful restoration by the great expert Clive Rous they should be on show to the public in 1979.

Erddig
Clwyd

By the nineteenth century, country-house life in England was admired, envied and imitated all over the world. There was nothing quite like it anywhere else. Historic old houses filled with treasures and surrounded by parks with herds of deer browsing under the great trees – moors to shoot on, rivers to fish in, stables full of horses, a well-stocked library and a billiard room for a rainy day, food in abundance, dozens of comfortable bedrooms for friends and relations – a pleasanter form of existence has seldom been devised.

Of course it was only made possible by large numbers of servants – by gardeners, grooms and gamekeepers in abundance, as well as servants actually in the house. The drawing-rooms, dining-rooms and bedrooms where the family who owned the house lived and entertained were only the upper half of the iceberg. Under the water-line, so to speak, was a quite different world and system. It was the world of the kitchen, laundry, dairy, brew-house, servants' hall, butler's pantry, housekeeper's room, backstairs, housemaids' closets, workshops, saw-pits, harness-room, coach-house, and so on. Up till the end of the nineteenth century most country houses were still largely self-sufficient. They baked their own bread, made their own jam, cured their own hams, brewed their own ale, washed their own laundry, and had their own craftsmen for repair and maintenance and for making all kinds of things from new gates for the farm to dolls' houses for the children.

At many country houses open to the public one gets little idea of this other world and how it lived and worked, but at Erddig one can explore it in fascinating detail. This is partly because the National Trust has taken endless time and trouble to put it all on show – even to the extent of bringing visitors in through the back yards and the servants' rooms, rather than the front door. But it is also because of the sort of people the Yorke family, who owned Erddig, were. Even more than other country house owners they seem never to have thrown anything away. And they had an unusual relationship with their servants.

The way families got on with their staff differed very widely from house to house. On the whole the tendency over the centuries was for the life of the family to be more and more divided from the life of the servants. Many families in the nineteenth century acted through their butler, head cook and housekeeper, and seldom spoke to or even saw the dozen or two dozen junior servants who worked under them. A kitchen maid could work for years in a big house without ever even seeing the drawing-room or family bedrooms. There were all sorts of

opposite preceding page The east front of Erddig. The roof of the original house, built in 1684–7, can be seen in the centre. Wings were added to either side in the 1720s.

preceding page Portraits and photographs preserved at Erddig include (from the top down) William Hughes, woodman; a negro coachboy; Edward Prince, carpenter; a nanny; Albert Gillam, gardener; a housekeeper.

left A detail in the saloon. To either side of a George III chandelier are gilt pier-glasses originally supplied in the 1720s for the two best bedrooms.

exceptions, and the children of the family tended to break through the barriers and make the whole system more human, but in general the traditional baize door which divided servants from family divided houses into two completely self-contained worlds.

The Yorkes at Erddig were very close to their servants however, and took a great interest in them. They even took more trouble over having their servants painted or photographed than themselves. In the 1790s Philip Yorke I (all Yorke sons were either Philip or Simon) had six portraits of his servants painted by John Walters of Denbigh and wrote verses to go with them (and with a delightful portrait of a negro coachboy who worked at Erddig earlier in the century). Three more portraits were painted in 1830, with verses by Simon Yorke II; then from 1852 the Yorkes moved over to photography. The portraits of servants hang in the servants' hall; the basement corridor outside it is lined with literally dozens of Victorian and Edwardian photographs of servants, in groups or individually, with attached verses mostly by Philip Yorke II. This kindly but eccentric squire seems to have burst into doggerel verse on every possible occasion. And so one learns that Nellie Rogers,

> For twelve years was all in all
> To the Young Ladies in the hall,

and how in the time of Albert Gillam,

> Ne'er did our borders look more gay
> Than they have done beneath his sway.

As for the coachman in 1886,

> His name, we recollect, was Meacock,
> And he was proud as any peacock.

The extraordinary thing about Erddig is that not only can one get to know these servants of long ago through their portraits and photographs, but one can then go out and look for the places in which they worked, and find them almost untouched, often still equipped with the actual tools and equipment they used, and sometimes with the clothes they wore still hanging on the wall. One can visit the blacksmith's and joiner's workshops, the sawpit, and the sawmill that partly replaced it, where the steam-engine of about 1860 which drove the saw is still in working order. There are ponderous Victorian mangles in the laundry, and the huge late eighteenth-century kitchen still has its original cupboards and dressers, and the inscription 'Waste not, Want not' prominently painted across one wall. In the stable yard all kinds of methods of transport are on view, including an Edwardian governess-cart, a Victorian 'bone-shaker' and a 1907 Rover. The Rover was the first car at Erddig. It was bought in the 1920s from the chimney-sweep – who had bought it from the vicar – and it was to be followed by 1924 and 1927 Austins, both still at Erdigg. The 1927 Austin remained the family car until

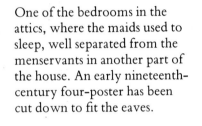

One of the bedrooms in the attics, where the maids used to sleep, well separated from the menservants in another part of the house. An early nineteenth-century four-poster has been cut down to fit the eaves.

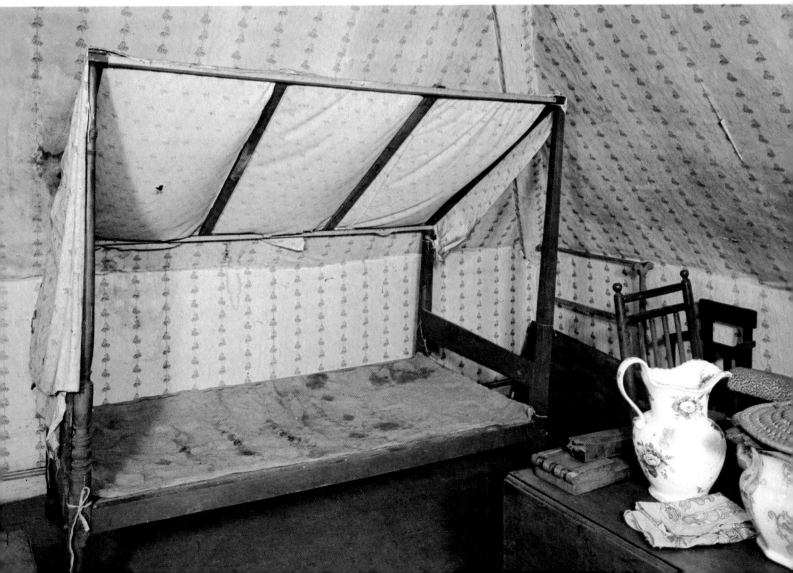

after the last war, when it was described as 'going well, but giving a bit of trouble in the second gear'.

Further inside the house is the estate office, off the corridor where the servants' photographs hang. It still has its rows of ledgers, tin boxes, bundles of estate plans and antique typewriter. In the butler's pantry the footmen's overcoats and livery are still hanging in a cupboard. As in other houses, a footman used to sleep in the pantry at night to keep watch on the silver in the safe. The National Trust have adapted several of the cupboards as show-cases, so that the silver is now on view in the room where the butler and footmen used to spend long hours polishing and guarding it. These show-cases are full of fine seventeenth- and eighteenth-century silver and introduce the other aspect of Erddig. The fact that nothing was ever thrown away or sold means that it is full of treasures, as well as survivals and oddities.

Erddig was originally built in the 1680s by a local landowner who went bankrupt before he had completed it. It was bought and enlarged by a successful London lawyer John Meller. He was a bachelor, and when he died in 1733 he left the property to his nephew Simon Yorke. The extent of the original house is

above A collection of bicycles in an outhouse in the stable yard. The 'bone-shaker' on the right belonged to Philip Yorke II, squire of Erddig in the late nineteenth century, and was made by J. Hill of Piccadilly.

right A model inspired by the Roman ruins at Palmyra in Syria, now on show in the gallery. It is faced with mother-of-pearl and was made in 1773 by Betty Ratcliffe, the lady's maid at Erddig.

shown by the roof which pushes up in the middle of the garden front. The squires of Erddig employed obscure local architects, or no architects at all, and the house is interesting for what is in it, not for its architecture: the best that one could say about the latter is that it is 'unassuming'.

When John Meller bought Erddig in 1716, he fitted it out with furniture and fittings bought in London. A remarkable amount of this is still at Erddig, and makes it one of the best country houses in England in which to study early eighteenth-century furniture. There are carved and gilded or silvered chairs and looking-glasses almost by the dozen, lacquered and japanned furniture and tapestries woven in Soho especially for Erddig; and there is the state bed. After careful restoration at the Victoria and Albert museum this now looks much as it must have done when Philip Hunt of 'Ye Looking Glass and Cabinet' in St Paul's churchyard first upholstered it with embroidered Chinese silk, and John Meller had it sent up to Erddig in 1720.

Apart from John Meller's many purchases, the house is crowded with objects of all kinds and periods from Chinese wallpapers and cupboards full of eighteenth-century porcelain to a Regency harp, a Victorian rocking-horse and a clutch of Edwardian teddy-bears. In all the strange and highly personal medley, nothing is stranger or more beautiful than the Chinese pagoda and Roman ruins made in mother-of-pearl by Elizabeth Ratcliffe, who was the lady's maid and companion of Mrs Yorke in the 1760s and 70s.

A downstairs room was used by the family as their 'museum' in Victorian and Edwardian days. Here the contents are strange but not at all beautiful; indeed visitors may wonder if they have ever seen a crazier mixture than the human skull, hornets' nest, stuffed birds, Egyptian tram tickets, broken pottery and old coins and weapons that are jumbled together in its show-cases. The museum is one of the last rooms to be visited; and by the time one gets there it is becoming clear that the Yorke family was a little eccentric.

English country houses have always bred a large number of eccentrics. A squire living in the middle of his two or three thousand acres was able to do more or less what he wanted, without bothering about what his neighbours thought of him. Some landowners were wildly and extravagantly crazy. The fifth Duke of Portland hated being seen by anyone, and built himself a vast warren of underground rooms and even an underground drive through his park. 'Mad Windham', at Felbrigg Hall in Norfolk, used to dress up as a ticket collector and punch everyone's tickets on the Norwich–London express. By these standards the Yorkes of Erddig were only gently eccentric, but they seem always to have been

left Simon Yorke IV and Philip Yorke III as children in about 1907. Philip Yorke gave Erddig to the National Trust in 1973. Years of neglect by his eccentric elder brother Simon had nearly led to its destruction.

unlike the neighbouring squires along the Welsh border. They didn't hunt or shoot; from the eighteenth century many of them were vegetarians; and their passion for hoarding certainly went beyond normal limits.

In the end, their eccentricity nearly finished Erddig. Simon Yorke IV, who owned Erddig from 1922 to 1966, had a bitter quarrel with the Coal Board; the house had been badly damaged through subsidence caused by colliery workings directly underneath it, and in the end he let the whole place become derelict while continuing to live in it. Water poured through the ceiling, down the canopy of the state bed, and lay in pools on the dining-room floor, so that he had to eat his meals in gumboots. Sheep wandered into the saloon and gazed at their reflections in the Queen Anne mirrors. The gardens became an impenetrable wilderness.

When Simon died in 1966 his brother Philip inherited a house and property in an apparently hopeless state of decay, but fortunately he and the National Trust (to whom he gave Erddig in 1972) refused to despair. Negotiations with the Coal Board led to the payment of a very large sum as compensation for damage; and after several years of careful restoration, Erddig has risen from its ruins to delight and fascinate visitors for many generations to come.

End March–October: daily (except Monday) 12–5.30, Bank Holiday Mondays 12–5.30. No admission after 4.30. Refreshments available.

Uppark
Sussex

Uppark

Sussex

Uppark is one of the most attractive houses in England. Everything about it is a little different from other houses. The first difference is its position. To reach it involves a climb of five hundred feet through the beech woods of the South Downs, up and up a long steep hill. When the house finally appears one doesn't fully appreciate its situation; all that is visible is a comfortable, welcoming old house at the end of a tree-enclosed approach. It isn't until one walks round to the other side that one realizes it is on top of the world – right on top of the downs, with the green turf coming up to its walls and a huge undulating view gradually sinking towards a glimpse of the sea in the far distance.

Another special feature of Uppark is its colour. Whether this is the result of its exposed position, and the salt of the sea breezes, or because inside and out the original materials have never been replaced, the colours at Uppark are a continual joy. The bricks – all just a little different from each other, as is usually the case with hand-made bricks – have mellowed to a silvery pink. Inside, almost none of the fabrics has been renewed, and few of the rooms have even been repainted in the last hundred or two hundred years. The result is a peaceful harmony of faded ivory, crimson, pink and blue, gently dusted with gold.

The next difference is its history. Most country houses have at least one good story or romantic incident attached to them, but none has more than Uppark; it is a continuous fairy story, in which the prince marries the goose-girl, and the poor boy becomes rich beyond the dreams of avarice.

The story starts with a villain – Ford Grey, first Earl of Tankerville, who built the house in about 1690. He ran away with his wife's sister, intrigued with the Duke of Monmouth against James II, took part in Monmouth's disastrous rebellion in 1685, turned king's evidence, but finally abandoned James II in favour of William of Orange. This double-dealing career was rewarded by thirteen years of prosperity, during which he rebuilt the old house on the down in the Up Park, which he had inherited from his mother. His architect may have been William Talman, but the house was built according to a standard pattern of the time followed by country gentlemen all over England. It is a brick house three storeys high with wooden trim and a central pediment, the third storey lit by dormer windows in the roof. One can understand why the model was so popular: it produced comfortable, easy-going gentlemen's houses, not too large or overbearing, which were – and indeed still are – a pleasure to live in.

The next episode in the Uppark story starts in 1746. A rich London merchant

preceding page The south front of Uppark. The house was built in about 1690 by the Earl of Tankerville. The architect may have been William Talman who was later to design the south front of Chatsworth.

below Looking along the west front. The house is situated high on the Sussex downs, with superb views in three directions. Underground passages lead below the lawns to separate kitchen and stable blocks, added in the 1750s. Food was pushed on heated trolleys from the kitchen to the dining-room in the main block.

The dining-room retains its original late seventeenth-century panelling. According to legend, Emma Hart, later to become famous as Nelson's beloved mistress Emma Hamilton, once danced naked on the table. There is no doubt that she came to Uppark in 1780 as the mistress of its young owner Sir Harry Fetherstonhaugh.

called Sir Henry Fetherstonhaugh died childless and left his large fortune to a remote cousin, a poor but honest young man called Matthew Fetherstonhaugh, who lived in Newcastle. Two far from onerous conditions were attached to this agreeable legacy: Matthew had to buy a baronetcy and an estate in the south of England. Within a year he had become Sir Matthew Fetherstonhaugh, Bart., had married a pretty young wife, and had bought Uppark from Lord Tankerville's grandson.

The next twenty-five years must have been very pleasant ones for Sir Matthew and Lady Fetherstonhaugh. Sir Matthew became a member of parliament; the family toured the continent, using their new fortune to buy pictures and furniture; they had their portraits painted in Rome; they built themselves a grand London house in Whitehall, and altered and redecorated Uppark. The delicate plasterwork ceilings and marble chimney-pieces, as well as most of the contents of the main rooms date from their time. Another of their contributions was more utilitarian. By the mid-eighteenth century it had become fashionable to keep servants and everything to do with them as invisible as possible. Accordingly, the kitchens, stables and other servants' rooms at Uppark were removed to two separate buildings. These are about fifty yards to either side of the house, and apparently not connected to it. In fact, long cavernous top-lit tunnels join them to the basement. Charcoal-heated trolleys used to trundle the food along these tunnels, from the enormous, now long-disused, eighteenth-century kitchens, which still contain their ponderous early stoves and other fittings.

Sir Matthew died in 1774, leaving a twenty-year-old heir, Harry. With all the money in the world, and the gay and dissolute society of the Prince Regent and Beau Brummel in which to spend it, Harry Fetherstonhaugh set out to enjoy himself. Racing, hunting and gambling filled his days. The gay and fashionable came flocking to Uppark for race-meetings, balls and midnight drives and picnics on the Downs. With a cellarful of wine, a stableful of horses and Emma Hamilton in his bedroom, Sir Harry became the epitome of the fashionable young Regency rake. Emma Hamilton, the future mistress of Nelson, was then still Emma Hart, aged only fifteen, a lusciously beautiful country girl from Cheshire who could scarcely read or write. Sir Harry probably found her in a night-club in London. She lasted a year at Uppark and then he sent her back to Cheshire, apparently in disgrace (but she soon recovered, found a new protector, married the British ambassador in Naples, and met Nelson). Many years later, after Nelson's death, she and Sir Harry conducted a friendly but very formal correspondence; no one could have guessed from it that she had once danced on the dining-room table at Uppark.

Sir Harry's fast and fashionable life continued after her departure. He struck up a friendship with the Prince Regent, who often came to stay at Uppark (his bed and bedroom there have not changed very much since he left them). Then something happened; nobody quite knows what, but Sir Harry wrote darkly about his 'great and numerous' enemies. His friendship with the Prince Regent came to a sudden end, and he retired from society.

The rows of stone pillars through which one now enters the house, and the long corridor behind it, date from this period. Sir Harry consoled himself in his retirement by changing the entrance from the side to the back, and otherwise tinkering with the house, with Humphry Repton as his architect. His alterations were on a modest scale; it seems likely that some of his troubles were financial ones. At one time he even considered selling Uppark to the great Duke of Wellington; but the duke saw the hill and decided against it.

Sir Harry's career had a final surprise in it. In 1825, when he was over seventy, he married his dairy-maid Mary Ann Bullock. Her dairy is still there, as untouched as everything else at Uppark, across the lawn from the main house. It has a verandah and two benches outside it, and a cool tiled interior in which, perhaps, the elderly Sir Harry grew over-excited at the sight of Mary Ann's buxom arms dipping into the cream. Mary Ann was sent off to Paris to be educated, and then Sir Harry married her in the saloon at Uppark. She and Sir Harry, her little sister Frances, and her sister's governess Miss Sutherland (who was rumoured to be Sir Harry's daughter) lived quietly on until Sir Harry died in 1846, aged ninety-two. He left Uppark and all its lands and contents to his wife; and when she died in 1874 she left it to her sister. Frances Bullock-Fetherstonhaugh (as she now called herself) never married. She lived alone at Uppark with her former governess, Miss Sutherland. The two old ladies always dressed in black velvet, because they thought it suited the house. They were proud that they preserved Uppark 'as Sir 'Arry 'ad it'. Miss Sutherland died in 1893 and Miss Bullock-Fetherstonhaugh two years later – a hundred and twenty-one years after her brother-in-law Sir 'Arry had inherited it from his father.

Now comes the next Uppark surprise. Not content with having Emma Hamilton dancing on the dining-room table, it had H. G. Wells chasing the maids along the kitchen tunnel. His mother Sarah Wells was housekeeper at Uppark from 1880 to 1893. Her snug and comfortable housekeeper's room survives intact in the basement, complete with a photograph of her. It shows a formidable lady encased in black satin, the epitome, one would have thought, of an old-fashioned housekeeper. According to her son, however, she was extremely inefficent; matters were not helped by the fact that she and Miss Bullock-Fetherstonhaugh were both deaf, and neither could hear what the other was saying. Miss Bullock-Fetherstonhaugh had no relatives of her own (or at least none that she considered suitable for Uppark) and there were no obvious relatives of Sir Harry to whom the house should go. So once again it came out of the clouds to someone who wasn't expecting it. It was left by the terms of her will to the sons of two of her

right The saloon was redecorated in about 1770, and probably retains its original paintwork, now mellowed to a gentle grey and gold. It looks through five long windows over the downs. The chairs were made for Uppark in 1771, by Paul Saunders of Soho Square.

below Sir Harry Fetherstonhaugh and his dog, painted during a visit to Rome in 1776, by Pompeo Batoni.

neighbours – first to Colonel Keith Turnour, and after his death to Herbert Meade, the younger son of the Earl of Clanwilliam. He added Fetherstonhaugh to his name and ended his career in the navy as Admiral Sir Herbert Meade Fetherstonhaugh. It was he, jointly with his son, who gave Uppark to the National Trust in 1954.

Every country house has its own atmosphere, and none more so than Uppark. The sinister Lord Tankerville and the dashing Sir Harry have contributed little to it; there is nothing sinister or in the least bit rakish about it today. It has the comfortable old-fashioned feeling of an old ladies' house, in which everything is scoured and polished, nothing is allowed to get out of place, and tea with buttered scones is served exactly at five. But unlike most old ladies' houses the contents are all of museum quality; almost every object in every room is an example of eighteenth-century taste at its best and most discriminating; and yet the rooms don't feel like museum rooms.

Much of this atmosphere must come from the two old ladies in their black velvet, sitting all day in the little eighteenth-century parlour in the corner of the house, reading and sleeping and stroking their pet dogs, as H. G. Wells described them. Much, too, is due to Lady Meade Fetherstonaugh, the wife of the admiral.

above The famous Uppark doll's house was made and furnished in about 1730 for little Sarah Lethieullier, whose coat of arms is in the pediment. In 1746 she married Sir Matthew Fetherstonhaugh and came to live at Uppark, bringing her doll's house with her.

right The early nineteenth-century dairy. Sir Harry Fetherstonhaugh fell in love with his dairy-maid Mary Anne Bullock, and married her in 1825 when he was over seventy. He left the house to her on his death twenty-one years later.

170

End March–September:
Wednesday, Thursday, Sunday
and Bank Holiday Mondays
2–6. All visitors guided on
Wednesday.

When her husband inherited the house in 1931 she dedicated the rest of her life to recovering and restoring its eighteenth-century curtains, upholstery and wall coverings. The majority of these still survived, but many were hanging in rags and tatters. They were lovingly restored as a result of hours of patient labour by Lady Meade Fetherstonhaugh and her helpers; as an aid to the work she revived the use of the herb saponaria, which could be grown locally and has remarkable properties of bringing back life and colour to fabrics which are treated with it.

The last of the special surprises of Uppark is in the last of the rooms shown to visitors on the ground floor. It is the world-famous Uppark doll's house. This was brought to Uppark in 1747 by Lady Fetherstonhaugh, the wife of Sir Matthew. It was made for her as a child and must have sent her wild with excitement when she first saw it. It is a grand Georgian house in miniature with a row of statues along the top like a little palace. The front opens in sections, and each section reveals a set of rooms completely furnished down to the smallest detail, with dolls to match. The servants are in the kitchen, the cooking-pots on the fire, the baby in its cradle, the gentry taking tea in the drawing-room, fully dressed down to the last petticoat. Its untouched survival is as much of a miracle as the untouched survival of Uppark itself.

Penrhyn Castle
Gwynedd

It is every architect's dream to have a client who comes to him and says 'Build this for me, my boy. Do what you like. Money is no object.' It happens seldom enough, but it seems to have happened at Penrhyn Castle.

The client was George Hay Dawkins Pennant. He had been born George Hay Dawkins, and added on the 'Pennant' in 1808, when he inherited the Penrhyn estate and a vast fortune from his great-uncle Richard Pennant, Baron Penrhyn. Penrhyn had belonged to Richard Pennant's wife, formerly a Miss Anne Warburton, a descendant of John Williams, Archbishop of York, who had bought the estate in the early seventeenth century. There was nothing grand about the estate or the house in those days. The money was contributed by Richard Pennant and came from his Jamaican sugar plantations and Welsh slate quarries. He inherited the plantations from his father, but developed the quarries on his own initiative. They were in the Nant Ffrancon valley, which runs up into the mountains within sight of Penrhyn. Richard Pennant built a road up to them, and by the end of the eighteenth century the sea, navigable rivers and the new canal system enabled Welsh slate to be transported cheaply all over Britain. By the 1790s the quarries were exporting twelve thousand tons a year. The huge cliffs of slate cut deep into the mountainside, and dwarfing the quarry workers who swarmed like ants all over them, appealed to contemporary taste for the sublime and the mysterious, and attracted sightseers from all over the British Isles. The quarries supplied the Pennants with an enormous income, which grew more enormous every year.

Richard Pennant had brought the old house at Penrhyn mildly up to date. At the end of the eighteenth century it was already becoming fashionable to build in the gothic style, so he put in gothic windows and added a few battlements. Dawkins Pennant lived in the house for nearly twenty years without doing anything more to it. Then in about 1827, when he was sixty-four years old, he decided to turn it into a castle – the biggest castle in the British Isles after Windsor.

By then the novels of Walter Scott and other writers had made people castle-

left Looking along the north-west front to a distant view of Snowdonia. Penrhyn Castle was designed by Thomas Hopper for G.H. Dawkins Pennant, who derived an enormous fortune from his slate quarries and sugar plantations.

right The family wing at the southern end of the castle. It is closely copied from a Norman keep of the twelfth century, but was in fact built in the 1820s, like the rest of the castle.

conscious. Castles were admired because they were romantic and also because they were picturesque. People had become tired of symmetrical flat-topped buildings surrounded by formal gardens; they developed a taste for mountain scenery and the kind of rambling buildings with striking skylines which fitted in with a mountain background. The rich soon realized that they could live in castles as well as go and look at them. If they didn't own an old castle, they could build a new one. If they lived in an old castle which had been altered they could turn it back into a castle again. This is what George IV did at Windsor on a regal scale and inevitably the king's example was followed all over Britain.

There had never been a genuine medieval castle at Penrhyn. The Pennants were not an old family; Dawkins Pennant did not even have his uncle's remote connection with the Williamses who had bought Penrhyn in the seventeenth century. There was no obvious reason to turn Penrhyn into a castle except that castles were fashionable, and there were a lot of real ones in Wales already. Perhaps the recent origins of the Pennant wealth also had something to do with it. In every century one of the accepted ways for a new family to dig themselves into the upper classes has been to build a grand country house. The eleven towers, innumerable turrets and endless battlements of Penrhyn helped launch the Pennants into the aristocracy and disguised the fact that they were basically Liverpool merchants who had struck oil – or rather slate.

The transformation was effected for Dawkins Pennant by the architect Thomas Hopper. Hopper had been fashionable ever since George IV – then still Prince Regent – had commissioned a gothic conservatory from him in 1807. Like most architects at the time, he was prepared to design buildings in almost any style. He had already designed one castle in Ireland and altered another. His new Irish castle was at Gosford in County Armagh. It had the distinction of being the first of the new castles to be Norman. Either Hopper persuaded Dawkins Pennant, or Dawkins Pennant asked Hopper, to make Penrhyn Norman too. The reason was probably simple one-upmanship. By the 1820s there were plenty of new castles but only one other new Norman one, and that in a part of Ireland which relatively few people visited. Penrhyn was bound to be talked about.

The reason why most people steered clear of Norman was straightforward. Norman was the oldest, most primitive and uncomfortable of the English styles (except of course Saxon, of which only a handful of churches, and no houses or castles, survived). It was hard enough to build something which looked

above Penrhyn from the air. The family wing in the keep is to the left, the main block in the centre, the stables and servants' wing to the right.

right The hall is like a section from a Norman cathedral, complete with stained glass. The upper row of arches open into the bedroom corridors.

below In the vaulted drawing-room massive Norman arches enclose the latest triumph of early nineteenth-century technology – huge mirrors each made from a single sheet of plate glass

sufficiently like a castle and was still reasonably comfortable without loading the dice against oneself by making it Norman too.

This was the challenge which Hopper faced. He had the advantage of one of the best sites in the British Isles. From its hillside platform Penrhyn has a view of breathtaking beauty. Looking east from the terrace before the house, the sea and Puffin Island are down below to the left; in front is the long line of the Welsh coast; to the right is the whole grand mass of Snowdonia. Presented with this site and with apparently unlimited access to the Pennant millions, Hopper set out to enjoy himself.

To build a Norman castle in the 1820s was an almost impossible, not to say absurd, task. But Hopper clearly had such fun carrying it out, showed such ingenuity in solving all the problems, and let himself go with such abandon, that the result is intensely enjoyable. The Normans had tiny windows with no glass in them; they had cramped circular stone staircases and very little furniture; they scarcely had tapestry, let alone panelling or plastered walls or wallpaper. Their castles were draughty, cold, dark and dirty. Hopper had to make it all up as he went along, but nothing daunted him. He designed Norman wallpaper, Norman carpets, Norman washstands, Norman firescreens, a Norman billiard-table, Norman sash windows, sideboards, sky-lights and sofas – and a Norman grand staircase. Of course he had to cheat a bit. Much of his detail is derived from Norman churches and cathedrals rather than castles. The plaster ceilings are covered with writhing ornament inspired by Anglo-Saxon manuscripts. Most of the furniture isn't Norman, but it is all suitably massive, and almost all covered in decoration.

The normal arrangement for a genuine Norman castle was the 'motte-and-

left The Norman arches in the library are as massive and elaborately decorated as anything in the house, but their barbaric richness is combined with musical instruments, writing-tables, a billiard-table, fireplaces, books and all the requirements of a luxurious nineteenth-century house.

right The architect had to invent his own Norman-style grand staircase, since nothing of that nature existed in real Norman castles or cathedrals. He let himself go, with amazing results.

bailey' plan. There was a tall heavily-fortified keep on a 'motte' or mound at one end, and stretching out from it one or more courts or baileys enclosed by fortified walls. Hopper cleverly adapted this arrangement for Penrhyn. The keep on its motte became a private wing for the Pennant family; a kitchen court and a stables court corresponded to an inner and an outer bailey. In between the motte and the baileys Hopper infiltrated what was in fact a large and comfortable nineteenth-century house in which the Pennants could entertain enormous house-parties – although the entire building was heavily disguised in Norman fancy dress. The whole vast conglomeration stretches along the hillside for more than 600 feet.

In fact, although the detail is all more or less Norman, the general shape of most of the towers and turrets is inspired by later medieval castles. But medieval castles of all dates were mainly designed for practical reasons – the towers were where they were because they helped fortify the castle to the best advantage. Hopper worked everything out so that it would look good. The silhouette of the skyline and the way the towers group together is all exactly calculated for the best possible effect, like a series of brilliant stage sets.

Hopper showed the same eye for scenery inside the house. The massive front door leads into a long and comparatively low vaulted corridor, which makes visitors' final emergence into the great hall all the more dramatic. The great hall has a stone vault, rises the whole height of the castle, and is sombrely lit through glowing stained glass windows. It is more like a section of a Norman cathedral than anything in a genuine Norman castle – except that what would have been the triforium galleries in a cathedral have been turned into bedroom passages. It leads to the library where there are more church-like arches and a riot of Norman-style ornament covering every square inch of wall and ceiling. After these two extraordinary rooms the drawing-room and dining-room seem relatively conventional, apart from their enormous size. But the main staircase is yet another *tour de force*. It starts off dark and confined, with flights of stone steps weaving their way through richly ornamented stone arches. But at the top it breaks into brightly-lit spaciousness, culminating in a ceiling in which Hopper really let himself go. It is an amazing mixture of writhing Celtic ornament, a perpendicular gothic fan vault with Norman panelling, and a sky-light adapted from a cathedral rose-window.

At the top of the staircase is the state bedroom in which Queen Victoria slept when she stayed at Penrhyn in 1859. Its Norman four-poster is the most splendid

left In the slate bedroom the bed is made of solid slate. The picture over the fireplace shows the nearby slate quarries which produced both the bed and the money to build Penrhyn.

bed at Penrhyn, but the most curious is undoubtedly the slate bed on show in another bedroom. This four-poster advertisement for the Pennant quarries is entirely made of slate (except the springs and mattress!) and weighs over a ton. Penrhyn also boasts a slate chimney-piece in the dining-room, an elaborately carved slate side-table in the hall and a slate billiard-table in the library. All billiard-tables have a slate bed below the cloth, but the Penrhyn table has polished slate legs and framework as well.

A few of the rooms at Penrhyn are on the dark side, but otherwise it was designed for comfort from the start. A deep well in the icehouse tower on the northern corner of the castle preserved all summer long the ice which had been brought by sea to the port below the castle, and packed into the well in the winter. In winter hot air gushed from wall and floor gratings in the hall and elsewhere on the ground floor and rose up into the bedroom corridors, while coal burned brightly in all the innumerable fireplaces. The library has hot-air gratings and no less than four fireplaces, one in each of its divisions.

The library was the room round which early nineteenth-century house-parties centred in all big country houses. The Penrhyn library was equipped with every variety of book, writing-tables, games and portfolios of prints and drawings, as well as the slate billiard-table. In bad weather guests could dig themselves into the various sections, with the fires hospitably blazing, and keep themselves amused all day. Houses like Penrhyn must be visualized filled with the house-parties for which they were designed. Penrhyn was given to the National Trust in 1951, but large house-parties continued to be given on a lavish scale up to the last war; and guests seem to have enjoyed the house then as much as visitors do today.

End March–October: daily 2–5, Bank Holiday Mondays 11–5. June–September: weekdays 11–5, weekends 2–5. Grounds close at 6. Tea room.

Lindisfarne Castle
Northumberland

Lindisfarne Castle
Northumberland

At some stage or other almost everyone dreams of living in a castle, but not many people manage to turn the dream into reality. In 1901 Edward Hudson, the owner and founder of *Country Life*, found himself with the chance of a lifetime. When driving with a friend in Northumberland he came, almost by chance, on an empty castle – no run-of-the-mill castle, but a castle growing out of the top of a crag like the ones in fairy stories. It was in no ordinary place either, but on a wild island next to a ruined abbey. The castle buildings were semi-derelict and had been much altered, which gave him an excellent excuse to employ the best architect in England to restore and remodel them.

Holy Island (or Lindisfarne, as it was originally called) was the base from which Christianity was brought to the north of England. St Aidan, followed by St Cuthbert, founded a monastery there in the eighth century, and made it famous all over Europe for holiness and learning. Then the Danes started to raid, rob and burn all along the coast, and in 875 the monks were forced to leave Lindisfarne Abbey. For two centuries the island was uninhabited, but in 1082 the Benedictines founded a new monastery on the site of the old one, and its ruins are still there today.

In 1537 the monastery, like all English monasteries, was closed down by Henry VIII. The island ceased to be a holy place and became a military stronghold. It had an excellent harbour; and a few hundred yards from the sheltered dip in the sand dunes where the monks had built their monastery was a hundred-foot-high crag, ideal for fortification. Here, thousands of years earlier, a jet of red-hot dolerite had forced its way through a crack in the sandstone, and then cooled and petrified.

The Danes had long ago ceased their raiding, but their place had been taken by the Scots. Lindisfarne was within a few miles of the Scottish border, and the harbour was used by the English fleet when it went on expeditions against Scotland. In about 1550 a small fort was built on top of the crag and garrisoned with a captain, two master gunners, a master's mate and twenty soldiers.

The union of England and Scotland put an end to Lindisfarne's function as a border fortification, but it played some part in the civil wars of the seventeenth century. In 1635 a visitor described it as a 'dainty little fort', and Captain Rugg, its governor, was 'as famous for his generous and free entertainment of strangers as for his great bottle nose, which is the largest I have seen'. A garrison was kept in the fort until the mid-eighteenth century, although there was little or nothing for it to do, except during a couple of days' excitement in the Jacobite revolt of 1715. It was removed in the mid-nineteenth century. The castle became a coastguard station, but by the time Hudson first saw it (climbing over the wall to do so) even the coastguards had gone.

The castle was and is still approached by a causeway from the mainland. At high tide the sea races across the sand flats and cuts the island off completely. Much of the land consists of sand dunes, but there are fields round the fishing village which grew up in the shade of the abbey buildings. The island is almost flat, except for its south-eastern tip, where the jagged castle crag sticks up dramatically by the sea shore.

When Hudson acquired the building it was more of a blockhouse than a castle, an unromantic building in a romantic position. He brought in Edwin Lutyens to make the building romantic as well. But the Edwardian way of being romantic was quite different from the early nineteenth-century one. Fancy-dress castles like Penrhyn, bristling with turrets and fortifications which were never meant to be

preceding page Lindisfarne Castle from the foreshore to the east. In the early 1900s Sir Edwin Lutyens remodelled the old fort for Edward Hudson, the owner of *Country Life*. It is entered by way of a steep causeway along the side of the cliff.

right A crooked, stepped passage slopes downwards from the entrance hall to the dining-room, seen here with its eighteenth-century Windsor chairs and the oval oak table specially designed for it by Luytens.

below Old beds, whitewashed walls and simple furnishings give the bedrooms a distinctive atmosphere. Every room has a superb view through little casement windows over the surrounding sea and coastline.

used, had gone out of fashion. Cultured Edwardians found them rather ridiculous. Lutyens made his buildings romantic not by making them assume another identity but by using local materials in a way that expressed the spirit of the surrounding landscape.

When he built houses in a comfortable south-of-England landscape, nestling in fields, woods and orchards, he built them of mellow brick and massive grey timbers. He planted creepers to grow all over them, and made them merge gently into terraces and gardens. But Lindisfarne was designed as a stone house that would seem to grow naturally out of its grey rock, and look strong and sturdy and capable of coping with the sea gales. It is sturdy and simple inside too; there is very little ornament, but walking round the house is made romantic and exciting by great stone arches and columns, and unexpected changes of direction and flights of winding stone steps.

The castle has wonderful views in all directions, but Lutyens was not the kind of architect to react to these in the obvious way, by constructing picture-windows through which to take everything in. Instead one comes on the views unexpectedly, when looking through little leaded windows from a stone window seat cut out of the thickness of a massive wall. It is only out on the terraces that the whole sweep of the prospect comes into view.

Lutyens largely rebuilt the actual castle buildings, but he kept the approach and the two massively fortified platforms or 'batteries' on which the cannon had originally stood. These are on two levels, and Lutyens designed the house so that hall, staircases and galleries would lead enticingly up from one level to the other. A steep approach ramp rises up the side of the cliff and burrows through the walls

and up a flight of steps to the lower battery. The ramp dates from the original castle, but Lutyens removed the parapet to make going up it more exciting.

The main part of the house looks over the lower battery, and is entered through a hall made almost cave-like by the massive pillars and arches which divide it into three parts. Beyond the hall are two even more cavernous stone-vaulted rooms. These are part of the original castle and were probably built as store-rooms for ammunition. Lutyens converted them into a dining-room and drawing-room (known as the 'ship room') by putting in fireplaces and cutting windows through the vaults.

From the lower level one can explore up the stone stairs to a long low gallery with bedrooms off it, and up yet more steps to one of the most desirable rooms in the castle – the upper gallery, originally a bedroom, which is on its own at the very top of the castle with little windows looking in all directions. From the main gallery one can emerge on to the spacious expanse of the upper battery to drink in the sea air, and lean over the parapet to survey sea and seaweed and sands stretching for miles below. On one side are the fields of the island with the village and abbey ruins beyond them. On the other is the bay and harbour, with two tall needle-like obelisks projecting unexpectedly out of the water to mark the navigation channel. In the distance, across the bay, is the romantic silhouette of Bamburgh Castle.

Edward Hudson used to fill the castle with guests. Asquith, the prime minister, came there with his daughter Lady Violet Bonham-Carter. So did Lord Baden-Powell, the founder of the Boy Scout movement, Sir Malcolm Sargent, the

above The castle as it was in the early nineteenth century. It was originally built in the 1540s, as a border fortification against the Scots. It later became a coastguard station, and was finally abandoned.

right Lutyens delighted in filling his houses with incident and surprise. The long gallery is reached by dark stone stairs leading out of the hall, and gives access to most of the bedrooms. The windows on the left open on to a sunny terrace, part of the original fortifications.

Massive stone columns and arches divide the hall, and make an exciting entrance to the castle. The furnishings have changed very little since the days of Edward Hudson, the first owner.

conductor, Madame Markova, the ballet dancer, and Madam Suggia, the greatest cellist of her day. When the latter played her cello in the castle it is said that the islanders used to gather on the rocks below to listen to her.

Not all visitors were enthusiastic. Lytton Strachey, the historian, described the castle as 'very dark, with nowhere to sit, and nothing but stone under, over and round you, which produces a distressing effect'. Even Lutyens's own wife complained that the fires smoked and that the castle was cold, and dangerous for small children. One can see what they meant – though one must remember that the castle was designed as a summer-holiday house for a bachelor. Lutyens's houses tend to be enjoyable to explore and wander round, rather than comfortable and convenient to live in. There really isn't anywhere to sit, the drawing-room must always have been dark and depressing, and the gallery, pleasant though it is, is too much of a passage. Much the most habitable room in the castle is the kitchen, the domain of Mr and Mrs Jack Lilburn and subsequently of their son and daughter, who looked after the castle from Hudson's time until 1968.

Hudson sold the castle in 1921. For many years it was the holiday home of Sir Edward de Stein, a merchant banker, and his sister, nephews, nieces and friends. He gave it to the National Trust in 1944, but continued to use it for holidays. The castle is furnished much as he left it. A good deal of the furniture dates in fact from Hudson's time. Some pieces were designed by Lutyens; but there is furniture and furnishings of other periods as well. Solid old Dutch cupboards, four-poster beds, tapestries, old clocks and prints, good carpets on the tiled floors, all combine to give one an impression of the people who lived there and the world they lived in. They suggest people with cultivated tastes and enough money to free them from worry, who lived in comfort but not luxury in a secure and leisurely world where the roads were still empty and they could drive peacefully round England and Europe, exploring old buildings and visiting their friends.

End March–September: daily (except Friday) 11–1 and 2–5.

Acknowledgments

Airviews: 98

John Bethell: *Title page*, 16–17 *top*, 26 *top*, 145, 153 *top*, 164, 169

Brighton Borough Council: 24, 25 *top*, 27, 31

British Tourist Authority: *Contents* (d), 18 *bottom left*, 59, 63, 68, 119, 138–9

Peter Burton: 64–5, 70–1 *top*

Country Life: 9, 13 *top, bottom left* and *right*, 28, 30, 43 *right* (A. Starkey), 66, 92, 93, 94, 95, 159 (a)

Department of the Environment: 19, 20, 21, 22 *top left*

Derbyshire Countryside Ltd: 60, 61, 62, 65

Kerry Dundas: 72 *bottom*

His Grace the Duke of Marlborough: 102

Robert Harding Associates: 48

Angelo Hornak: 16–17 *bottom*, 73, 100 *top*

Jarrolds: *Contents* (b), 32, 33, 34, 35, 36, 37, 38–9, 53, 54–5, 56 *top*, 56–7, 57 *top*, 58, 88–9, 180–1 *bottom*, 181 *top*, 183, 184

A.F.Kersting: *Contents* (a), 14–15, 40, 41, 45, 46–7, 74, 81, 84 *top*, 84–5, 91 *top*, 97, 127, 142 *bottom left*, 151, 154 *top*, 156, 173

E.Lamb (Castle Howard): 72 *top*

Lucinda Lambton: 67, 71 *right*, 96, 99, 105 *inset*, 106–7, 108, 108–9, 109, 110, 111

R.E.Lassam (Curator, Fox Talbot Museum): 140 *top*

National Portrait Gallery: 11, 127 *inset*, 133 *inset*

National Trust: *Endpapers, Contents* (c), 10, 88 *inset*, 90–1, 119 *inset*, 121, 122, 123, 124 *left and right*, 125, 126, 128, 129, 130, 131, 132, 133, 135, 136, 137, 141, 143 *right*, 144, 146, 148–9 *top*, 149 *bottom*, 150 *left*, 158, 159 (b–f), 160, 161, 162–3, 163 *right*, 165, 166, 167, 168, 170, 171, 172, 174, 174–5 *bottom*, 175 *top*, 176, 177, 178, 179, 182

Edward Piper: 142 *top*

Pilgrim Press Ltd: 75, 77, 78 *left and right*, 79, 80

Science Museum, London: 140 *bottom*

Scottish Tourist Board: 112

Edwin Smith: *Half-title*, 50 *top*, 50–1, 51 *top*, 52

Trans-Globe: 49 *bottom*, 70 *bottom left*, 104

Jeremy Whitaker: 42, 42–3, 44 *left and right*, 49 *top*, 83, 85 *top*, 86, 97 *inset*, 100–1 *bottom*, 101 *top*, 102 *top*, 103, 105, 142–3 *bottom*, 147, 148 *bottom*, 150 *right*, 157

Weidenfeld and Nicolson: 25 *bottom*

Woodmansterne: 112 *inset* (Clive Friend FIIP), 114 (Howard C. Moore), 115, 116, 117 (Nicholas Servian FIIP), 118 (Clive Friend FIIP)

The line diagram on page 40 was drawn by the author. For the illustration on page 152 we are grateful to the artist John Sambrook. It first appeared in *English Architecture, An Illustrated Glossary* by James Stevens Curl, David and Charles, 1977. The engravings on pages 18 and 69 first appeared in *Théâtre de la Grande Bretagne* by Kip and Kuyff and *Vitruvius Britannicus* respectively. Route maps based on the Automobile Association Five Mile series. Based on Ordnance Survey maps, with the permission of the Controller of H.M. Stationery Office. Crown Copyright Reserved.